The Ultimate

NINJA FOODI XL PRO

AIR FRYER OVEN

COOKBOOK

200 TASTY, HEALTHY AND AFFORDABLE AIR FRY OVEN RECIPES FOR EVERYONE TO AIR FRY, ROAST, BROIL, TOAST, DEHYDRATE AND MORE

DOMINGO CORONA

CONTENTS

INTRODUCTION..9

How the Ninja Foodi XL Pro Air Fryer Oven Works 9

The Benefits of the Ninja Foodi XL Pro Air Fryer Oven 9

The Preparations for the Ninja Foodi XL Pro Air Fryer Oven 9

How to Clean Your Ninja Foodi XL Pro Air Fryer Oven......................................10

BREAKFAST 12

French Toast 12

Bacon, Broccoli And Swiss Cheese Bread Pudding..12

Not-so-english Muffins 13

Pancake Muffins..13

Make-ahead Currant Cream Scones 14

Creamy Bacon + Almond Crostini 14

Orange-glazed Pears 15

Breakfast Bars..15

Sam's Maple Raisin Bran Muffins 16

Cheddar-ham-corn Muffins 16

Orange Rolls 17

Individual Overnight Omelets 17

Blueberry Muffins 18

Stromboli..18

Best-ever Cinnamon Rolls..19

Cherries Jubilee 20

Cheddar Bacon Broiler 21

Lemon Blueberry Scones 21

Strawberry Pie 22

Western Omelet 22

Bacon Cheddar Biscuits..22

Espresso Chip Muffins..23

Cinnamon Sugar Donut Holes..23

Zucchini Walnut Bread 24

Breakfast Pita 24

FISH AND SEAFOOD 26

Baked Clam Appetizers 26

Fish Tacos With Jalapeño-lime Sauce..26

Mediterranean Baked Fish 27
Almond Crab Cakes 27
Chilled Clam Cake Slices With Dijon Dill Sauce 28
Roasted Pepper Tilapia 28
Crunchy And Buttery Cod With Ritz® Cracker Crust 29
Flounder Fillets 29
Pecan-crusted Tilapia 29
Maple-crusted Salmon 30
Tuna Nuggets In Hoisin Sauce 30
Fish Sticks For Kids 31
Shrimp & Grits 31
Tasty Fillets With Poblano Sauce 32
Romaine Wraps With Shrimp Filling 32
Spiced Sea Bass 33
Lemon-dill Salmon Burgers 33
Shrimp Po'boy With Remoulade Sauce 34
Lemon-roasted Fish With Olives + Capers 34
Bacon-wrapped Scallops 35
Snapper With Capers And Olives 35
Sesame-crusted Tuna Steaks 35
Spicy Fish Street Tacos With Sriracha Slaw 36
Shrimp 37
Crab Cakes 37

LUNCH AND DINNER **39**
Chicken Noodle Soup 39
Light Beef Stroganoff 39
Baked French Toast With Maple Bourbon Syrup 40
Fillets En Casserole 40
Roasted Vegetable Gazpacho 40
Italian Stuffed Zucchini Boats 41
Connecticut Garden Chowder 42
Chicken Gumbo 42
Individual Chicken Pot Pies 42
Slow Cooker Chicken Philly Cheesesteak Sandwich 43
Honey-glazed Ginger Pork Meatballs 44
Miso-glazed Salmon With Broccoli 45
Favorite Baked Ziti 45

Pork And Brown Rice Casserole 46

One-step Classic Goulash 46

Scalloped Corn Casserole 47

Salad Couscous 47

Rosemary Lentils 48

Sheet Pan Loaded Nachos 48

Family Favorite Pizza 49

Kasha Loaf 49

Easy Oven Lasagne 50

Baked Parsleyed Cheese Grits 50

Herbal Summer Casserole 50

Oven-baked Barley 51

SNACKS APPETIZERS AND SIDES **52**

Beet Chips 52

Elote 52

Cheese Straws 53

Arancini With Sun-dried Tomatoes And Mozzarella 53

Broiled Maryland Crabcakes With Creamy Herb Sauce 54

Warm And Salty Edamame 55

Baked Brie And Cranberry Bites 55

Spinach And Artichoke Dip 55

Breaded Zucchini 56

Polenta Fries With Chili-lime Mayo 56

Eggs In Avocado Halves 57

Beef Satay With Peanut Dipping Sauce 57

Sweet Plantain Chips 58

Caramelized Onion Dip 59

Crispy Tofu Bites 60

Chicken Shawarma Bites 60

Savory Sausage Balls 60

Sugar-glazed Walnuts 61

Fried Green Tomatoes 61

Sausage Cheese Pinwheels 62

Fried Mozzarella Sticks 62

Cinnamon Pita Chips 63

Parmesan Crisps 63

Korean "fried" Chicken Wings 64

Golden Fried Cauliflower 64

POULTRY **66**

Peanut Butter-barbeque Chicken 66

East Indian Chicken 66

Crispy Duck With Cherry Sauce 67

Gluten-free Nutty Chicken Fingers 67

Chicken Chunks 68

Fiesta Chicken Plate 69

Chicken Pot Pie 69

Foiled Rosemary Chicken Breasts 70

Chicken Wellington 70

Fried Chicken 71

Tender Chicken Meatballs 72

Tasty Meat Loaf 72

Tandoori Chicken Legs 72

Roast Chicken 73

Curry Powder 73

Italian Roasted Chicken Thighs 74

Jerk Chicken Drumsticks 74

Crispy "fried" Chicken 75

Coconut Chicken With Apricot-ginger Sauce 75

Hot Thighs 76

Buffalo Egg Rolls 76

Marinated Green Pepper And Pineapple Chicken 77

Orange-glazed Roast Chicken 78

Roasted Game Hens With Vegetable Stuffing 78

Chicken Potpie 78

DESSERTS **80**

Mississippi Mud Brownies 80

Cheese Blintzes 80

Cowboy Cookies 81

Almond-roasted Pears 81

Green Grape Meringues 82

Lime Cheesecake 82

Giant Oatmeal–peanut Butter Cookie 83

Currant Carrot Cake 84

Goat Cheese–stuffed Nectarines 84

Individual Peach Crisps 84

Make-ahead Chocolate Chip Cookies 85

Brown Sugar Baked Apples 86

Scones 86

Peach Cobbler 87

Keto Cheesecake Cups 87

Lemon Torte 88

Soft Peanut Butter Cookies 88

Carrot Cake 89

Campfire Banana Boats 89

Cinnamon Sugar Rolls 90

Frozen Brazo De Mercedes 90

Coconut Rice Pudding 91

Graham Cracker Crust 92

Sweet Potato Donut Holes 92

Fried Snickers Bars 92

VEGETABLES AND VEGETARIAN **94**

Zucchini Boats With Ham And Cheese 94

Roasted Garlic Potatoes 94

Fried Cauliflowerwith Parmesan Lemon Dressing 95

Sesame Carrots And Sugar Snap Peas 95

Roasted Ratatouille Vegetables 96

Roasted Herbed Shiitake Mushrooms 96

Roasted Heirloom Carrots With Orange And Thyme 96

Rolled Chinese (napa) Cabbage With Chickpea Filling 97

Lentil-stuffed Zucchini 97

Steakhouse Baked Potatoes 98

Grits Casserole 98

Classic Baked Potatoes 99

Roasted Root Vegetables With Cinnamon 99

Roasted Belgian Endive With Pistachios And Lemon 99

Baked Mac And Cheese 100

Perfect Asparagus 100

Asparagus Fries 101

Salt And Pepper Baked Potatoes 101

Tandoori Cauliflower 101

Potatoes Au Gratin 102

Grits Again 102

Brown Rice And Goat Cheese Croquettes 103

Simply Sweet Potatoes 103

Roasted Corn Salad 104

Mushrooms, Sautéed 104

BEEF PORK AND LAMB **105**

Meatloaf With Tangy Tomato Glaze 105

Smokehouse-style Beef Ribs 105

Skirt Steak Fajitas 106

Herbed Lamb Burgers 107

Classic Pepperoni Pizza 107

Spicy Flank Steak With Fresh Tomato-corn Salsa 108

Steak With Herbed Butter 108

Perfect Pork Chops 109

Kielbasa Chunks With Pineapple & Peppers 109

Pretzel-coated Pork Tenderloin 109

Lime And Cumin Lamb Kebabs 110

Barbecue-style London Broil 110

Beef Bourguignon 111

Pesto Pork Chops 112

Lamb Koftas Meatballs 112

Orange Glazed Pork Tenderloin 113

Beer-baked Pork Tenderloin 113

Beef And Spinach Braciole 113

Sweet Potato–crusted Pork Rib Chops 114

Bourbon Broiled Steak 115

Kielbasa Sausage With Pierogies And Caramelized Onions 115

Lamb Curry 116

Vietnamese Beef Lettuce Wraps 116

Slow Cooked Carnitas 117

Zesty London Broil 118

INTRODUCTION

How the Ninja Foodi XL Pro Air Fryer Oven Works

An air fryer works by rapidly circulating hot air and a small amount of oil to fry foods. The oil and air work in tandem, transferring heat both via conduction (the direct contact of the hot oil) and convection (the heavy rotation of hot air). In a wall oven or the oven of a range with convection, the air fry function works the same way.

The Benefits of the Ninja Foodi XL Pro Air Fryer Oven

An air frying oven uses little to no oil to create a flavorful and crunchy texture on foods and boasts all of the same benefits as a standalone air fryer - with some additional conveniences.

The air fry feature is integrated right into your oven, eliminating the need to store an extra appliance or take up valuable counter space.

An air frying oven has more capacity, saving you time and allowing you to cook more food at once so that there's always enough for the whole family.

An air fry oven does more than just air fry, so one appliance works harder for you. Enjoy other features such as Even Baking with True Convection, Fast Steam Cleaning, and Smudge-Proof Stainless Steel.

The Preparations for the Ninja Foodi XL Pro Air Fryer Oven

1. Find the right place for your air fryer oven in your kitchen. Make sure you have some clearance around the oven so that the hot air can escape from the vent at the back.
2. Preheat your air fryer before adding your food. Because an air fryer heats up so quickly, it isn't critical to wait for the oven to preheat before putting food inside, but it's a good habit to get into. Sometimes a recipe requires a hot start and putting food into a less than hot oven will give you less than perfect results. For instance, pastry bakes better if cold pastry is placed into a hot oven. Pizza dough works better with a burst of heat at the beginning of baking. It only takes a few minutes to preheat the oven, so unless you're in a real rush, just wait to put your food inside.
3. Invest in a kitchen spray bottle. Spraying oil on the food is easier than drizzling or brushing, and allows you to use less oil overall. It will be worth it!
4. Think about lining your drip tray with aluminum foil for easy clean up.

How to Clean Your Ninja Foodi XL Pro Air Fryer Oven

After we have all the basic knowledge about the air fryer toaster ovens, let's discuss the very common question; how to clean a Cuisinart convection toaster oven, or how to clean a convection toaster oven? Following is a list of ways to clean it:

Clean it with homemade dish soap cleaner

For the best and safe cleaning, it is necessary to unplug your toaster oven and disconnect the apparatus from the force source before you start cleaning.

Also, obviously, never inundate it in water. After that, put the toaster oven on a bit of paper to get the pieces, then take out the metal plate, rack, and lower scrap plate and spot them in the sink. Then, use dish soap and water to wash these parts.

To battle any difficult stains on these removable pieces, and let them dry totally while you clean the remainder of the machine.

The next step is to make your own cleaning answer for the inside of the toaster oven by consolidating vinegar, warm water, and a little dish soap. Apply that to the inside with a clammy wipe.

However, do whatever it takes not to get any of the fluid on the warming components. Some toaster ovens have a porcelain polish or a nonstick inside that makes them marginally simpler to clean.

In any case, it very well may be harmed by metal scouring cushions and rough cleaners. You can utilize a wipe, material, or old cloth when cleaning down your toaster oven.

Clean it with baking soda

You might get surprised to know that how to clean a toaster oven with baking soda. Let us tell you the process in detail:

Baking Soda is incredible for cleaning since its normally antacid nature artificially responds to water and vinegar, which makes dirt and oil break down rapidly and without any problem.

Baking soda is an all-common substance present in every living thing. While the vast majority know it for baking, it's properties are extraordinary for a wide assortment of things.

It likewise has an incredible rough quality if not weakened excessively, so it's an extraordinary option in contrast to other markets since baking soda is an incredibly protected and powerful cleaning item.

Also, baking soda is totally non-poisonous and protected to use around food, children, and pets. You can also clean the heating component in your toaster oven by utilizing a gentle soap and a clean, buildup free cloth on a cool, unplugged toaster oven.

Tenderly wipe the loops guaranteeing no buildup from the cleaning cloth remains. Also, it is normal to have water and soap on the cloth; however, try not to get the radiator component significantly wet.

However, if we don't clear every ounce of buildup off, you'll get that delightful toasted baking soda smell whenever you use it. For another, we would prefer not to chance to harm the component, driving you to purchase another one.

Therefore, keep in mind that we have to unplug the toaster oven and do nothing until it's totally cool. Then, take a wipe or material in some warm water. Then start delicately cleaning the length of the warming component to and fro.

If you're following our entire how to clean a toaster oven with baking soda steps, this should be the first thing you do. As we said toward the beginning, try not to utilize soap or different cleaners on the warming components as they could harm it.

Try to let everything dry first prior to stopping the toaster oven back in or utilizing it. To clean a toaster oven with baking soda, make a glue with baking soda and water. In a cool, unplugged toaster oven, spread the glue within the oven, dodging the warming components.

Let it sit for 12 hours or more. For minor cleaning, 1 hour should do the trick, and then wipe clean with a soggy fabric and warm water. After that, we are well aware of the cleaning methods; let us understand the best way to turn off the digital air fryer.

BREAKFAST

French Toast

Servings: 4

Cooking Time: 40 Minutes

Ingredients:

- 2 eggs
- 1 cup skim milk or low-fat soy milk
- 1 tablespoon honey
- Salt
- 4 slices multigrain bread
- Vegetable oil

Directions:

1. Whisk together the eggs, milk, honey, and salt to taste in a shallow bowl. Add a bread slice to the mixture and let it soak for one minute. Carefully turn it over and let the liquid saturate the other side. With a spatula, place the bread slice in an oiled 6½ × 6½ × 2-inch square (cake) pan.

2. BROIL for 5 minutes, then turn carefully with a spatula and broil for another 5 minutes, or until golden brown. Repeat the soaking and broiling procedure for the remaining slices.

Bacon, Broccoli And Swiss Cheese Bread Pudding

Servings: 2

Cooking Time: 48 Minutes

Ingredients:

- ½ pound thick cut bacon, cut into ¼-inch pieces
- 3 cups brioche bread or rolls, cut into ½-inch cubes
- 3 eggs
- 1 cup milk
- ½ teaspoon salt
- freshly ground black pepper
- 1 cup frozen broccoli florets, thawed and chopped
- 1½ cups grated Swiss cheese

Directions:

1. Preheat the toaster oven to 400°F.

2. Air-fry the bacon for 6 minutes until crispy, rotate a few times while it cooks to help it cook evenly. Remove the bacon and set it aside on a paper towel.

3. Air-fry the brioche bread cubes for 2 minutes to dry and toast lightly. (If your brioche is a few days old and slightly stale, you can omit this step.)

4. Butter a 6- or 7-inch cake pan. Combine all the ingredients in a large bowl and toss well. Transfer the mixture to the buttered cake pan, cover with aluminum foil and refrigerate the bread pudding overnight, or for at least 8 hours.

5. Remove the casserole from the refrigerator an hour before you plan to cook, and let it sit on the countertop to come to room temperature.

6. Preheat the toaster oven to 330°F. Transfer the covered cake pan, to the air fryer oven, lowering the dish into the air fryer oven using a

sling made of aluminum foil (fold a piece of aluminum foil into a strip about 2-inches wide by 24-inches long). Fold the ends of the aluminum foil over the top of the dish before returning to the air fryer oven. Air-fry for 20 minutes. Remove the foil and air-fry for an additional 20 minutes. If the top starts to brown a little too much before the custard has set, simply return the foil to the pan. The bread pudding has cooked through when a skewer inserted into the center comes out clean.

Not-so-english Muffins

Servings: 4
Cooking Time: 10 Minutes

Ingredients:
- 2 strips turkey bacon, cut in half crosswise
- 2 whole-grain English muffins, split
- 1 cup fresh baby spinach, long stems removed
- ¼ ripe pear, peeled and thinly sliced
- 4 slices Provolone cheese

Directions:

1. Place bacon strips in air fryer oven and air-fry for 2minutes. Check and separate strips if necessary so they cook evenly. Air-fry for 4 more minutes, until crispy. Remove and drain on paper towels.

2. Place split muffin halves in air fryer oven and air-fry at 390°F for 2minutes, just until lightly browned.

3. Open air fryer oven and top each muffin with a quarter of the baby spinach, several pear slices, a strip of bacon, and a slice of cheese.

4. Air-fry at 360°F for 2minutes, until cheese completely melts.

Pancake Muffins

Servings: 4
Cooking Time: 8 Minutes

Ingredients:
- 1 cup flour
- 2 tablespoons sugar (optional)
- ½ teaspoon baking soda
- 1 teaspoon baking powder
- ¼ teaspoon salt
- 1 egg, beaten
- 1 cup buttermilk
- 2 tablespoons melted butter
- 1 teaspoon pure vanilla extract
- 24 foil muffin cups
- cooking spray
- Suggested Fillings
- 1 teaspoon of jelly or fruit preserves
- 1 tablespoon or less fresh blueberries; chopped fresh strawberries; chopped frozen cherries; dark chocolate chips; chopped walnuts, pecans, or other nuts; cooked, crumbled bacon or sausage

Directions:

1. In a large bowl, stir together flour, optional sugar, baking soda, baking powder, and salt.

2. In a small bowl, combine egg, buttermilk, butter, and vanilla. Mix well.

3. Pour egg mixture into dry ingredients and stir to mix well but don't overbeat.

4. Double up the muffin cups and remove the paper liners from the top cups. Spray the foil cups lightly with cooking spray.

5. Place 6 sets of muffin cups in air fryer oven. Pour just enough batter into each cup to cover the bottom. Sprinkle with desired filling. Pour in more batter to cover the filling and fill the cups about ¾ full.

6. Air-fry at 330°F for 8 minutes.

7. Repeat steps 5 and 6 for the remaining 6 pancake muffins.

Make-ahead Currant Cream Scones

Servings: 8
Cooking Time: 60 Minutes

Ingredients:
- 2 cups (10 ounces) all-purpose flour
- 3 tablespoons sugar
- 1 tablespoon baking powder
- ½ teaspoon table salt
- 5 tablespoons unsalted butter, cut into ¼-inch pieces and chilled
- ½ cup dried currants
- 1 cup heavy cream

Directions:
1. Adjust toaster oven rack to middle position and preheat the toaster oven to 375 degrees. Line large and small rimmed baking sheets with parchment paper.

2. Process flour, sugar, baking powder, and salt in food processor until combined, about 6 seconds. Scatter butter over top and pulse until mixture resembles coarse cornmeal with some slightly larger butter lumps, about 12 pulses. Transfer mixture to large bowl and stir in currants. Stir in cream with rubber spatula until dough begins to form, about 30 seconds.

3. Turn dough and any floury bits onto lightly floured counter and knead until rough, slightly sticky ball forms, 5 to 10 seconds. Shape dough into 8-inch round, about ¾ inch thick. Cut dough into 8 wedges.

4. Space desired number of scones at least 1 inch apart on prepared small sheet; space remaining scones evenly on prepared large sheet. Bake small sheet of scones until scone tops are light golden brown, 18 to 23 minutes. Transfer scones to wire rack and let cool for at least 10 minutes before serving.

5. Freeze remaining large sheet of scones until firm, about 1 hour. Transfer scones to 1-gallon zipper-lock bag and freeze for up to 1 month. To bake frozen scones, increase baking time to 20 to 25 minutes; do not thaw.

Creamy Bacon + Almond Crostini

Servings: 20
Cooking Time: 10 Minutes

Ingredients:
- 1 baguette loaf, cut into ½-inch-thick slices
- 2 tablespoons olive oil
- 4 ounces cream cheese, cut into cubes, softened
- ½ cup mayonnaise

- 1 cup shredded fontina cheese or Monterey Jack cheese
- 4 slices bacon, cooked until crisp and crumbled
- 1 green onion, white and green portions, finely chopped
- ¼ teaspoon Sriracha or hot sauce
- Dash kosher salt
- ¼ cup sliced almonds, toasted
- Minced fresh flat-leaf (Italian) parsley

Directions:

1. Toast the slices of the baguette in the toaster oven.

2. Arrange the toasted baguette slices on a 12-inch pizza pan or a 12 x 12-inch baking pan. Lightly brush the slices with the olive oil.

3. Preheat the toaster oven to 375°F.

4. Beat the cream cheese and mayonnaise in a medium bowl with an electric mixer at medium speed until creamy and smooth. Stir in the fontina, bacon, green onion, Sriracha, and salt and blend until combined.

5. Distribute the cheese mixture evenly over the toasted bread. Top with the sliced almonds. Bake for 6 to 8 minutes or until the cheese is hot and beginning to melt. Allow to cool for 1 to 2 minutes, then garnish with minced parsley. Serve warm.

Orange-glazed Pears

Servings: 4
Cooking Time: 19 Minutes

Ingredients:

- 2 ripe pears
- 1 tablespoon lemon juice
- 1 tablespoon margarine
- Pinch of salt
- Glaze:
- 2 tablespoons sugar
- 3 tablespoons orange juice

Directions:

1. Prepare the pears: peel, cut in half, remove the seeds and fibrous centers with a teaspoon, quarter and brush the pear pieces with the lemon juice, and set aside.

2. Combine the glaze ingredients in an oiled or nonstick 8½ × 8½ × 2-inch square baking (cake) pan.

3. BROIL for 4 minutes, or until the margarine is melted. Remove from the oven, stir to blend, add the pear quarters, and spoon the glaze mixture over the pears to coat well.

4. BROIL for 15 minutes, or until the glaze has thickened and the pears are tender and golden in color. Serve warm or chilled.

Breakfast Bars

Servings: 6
Cooking Time: 35 Minutes

Ingredients:

- 1 cup unsweetened applesauce
- 1 carrot, peeled and grated
- ½ cup raisins
- 1 egg
- 1 tablespoon vegetable oil
- 2 tablespoons molasses

- 2 tablespoons brown sugar
- ¼ cup chopped walnuts
- 2 cups rolled oats
- 2 tablespoons sesame seeds
- 1 teaspoon ground cinnamon
- ¼ teaspoon grated nutmeg
- ¼ teaspoon ground ginger
- Salt to taste

Directions:

1. Preheat the toaster oven to 375° F.

2. Combine all the ingredients in a bowl, stirring well to blend. Press the mixture into an oiled or nonstick 8½ × 8½ × 2inch square baking (cake) pan.

3. BAKE for 35 minutes, or until golden brown. Cool and cut into squares.

Sam's Maple Raisin Bran Muffins

Servings: 12
Cooking Time: 15 Minutes

Ingredients:

- 2 cups oat bran
- 2 teaspoons baking powder
- 2 eggs
- 1¼ cups low-fat soy milk
- ¾ cup raisins
- 3 tablespoons maple syrup
- 2 tablespoons vegetable oil
- Pinch of salt (optional)

Directions:

1. Preheat toaster oven to 425° F.

2. Combine all the ingredients in a bowl and stir until well blended. In a six-muffin 7 × 10 × 1½-inch tin, brush the pans with vegetable oil or use baking cups. Fill the pans or cups three-fourths full with batter.

3. BAKE for 15 minutes, or until a toothpick inserted in the center of a muffin comes out clean.

Cheddar-ham-corn Muffins

Servings: 8
Cooking Time: 8 Minutes

Ingredients:

- ¾ cup yellow cornmeal
- ¼ cup flour
- 1½ teaspoons baking powder
- ¼ teaspoon salt
- 1 egg, beaten
- 2 tablespoons canola oil
- ½ cup milk
- ½ cup shredded sharp Cheddar cheese
- ½ cup diced ham
- 8 foil muffin cups, liners removed and sprayed with cooking spray

Directions:

1. Preheat the toaster oven to 390°F.

2. In a medium bowl, stir together the cornmeal, flour, baking powder, and salt.

3. Add egg, oil, and milk to dry ingredients and mix well.

4. Stir in shredded cheese and diced ham.

5. Divide batter among the muffin cups.

6. Place 4 filled muffin cups in air fryer oven and bake for 5 minutes.

7. Reduce temperature to 330°F and bake for 1 to 2minutes or until toothpick inserted in center of muffin comes out clean.

8. Repeat steps 6 and 7 to cook remaining muffins.

Orange Rolls

Servings: 8

Cooking Time: 10 Minutes

Ingredients:

- parchment paper
- 3 ounces low-fat cream cheese
- 1 tablespoon low-fat sour cream or plain yogurt (not Greek yogurt)
- 2 teaspoons sugar
- ¼ teaspoon pure vanilla extract
- ¼ teaspoon orange extract
- 1 can (8 count) organic crescent roll dough
- ¼ cup chopped walnuts
- ¼ cup dried cranberries
- ¼ cup shredded, sweetened coconut
- butter-flavored cooking spray
- Orange Glaze
- ½ cup powdered sugar
- 1 tablespoon orange juice
- ¼ teaspoon orange extract
- dash of salt

Directions:

1. Cut a circular piece of parchment paper slightly smaller than the bottom of your air fryer oven. Set aside.

2. In a small bowl, combine the cream cheese, sour cream or yogurt, sugar, and vanilla and orange extracts. Stir until smooth.

3. Preheat the toaster oven to 300°F.

4. Separate crescent roll dough into 8 triangles and divide cream cheese mixture among them. Starting at wide end, spread cheese mixture to within 1 inch of point.

5. Sprinkle nuts and cranberries evenly over cheese mixture.

6. Starting at wide end, roll up triangles, then sprinkle with coconut, pressing in lightly to make it stick. Spray tops of rolls with butter-flavored cooking spray.

7. Place parchment paper in air fryer oven, and place 4 rolls on top, spaced evenly.

8. Air-fry for 10minutes, until rolls are golden brown and cooked through.

9. Repeat steps 7 and 8 to cook remaining 4 rolls. You should be able to use the same piece of parchment paper twice.

10. In a small bowl, stir together ingredients for glaze and drizzle over warm rolls.

Individual Overnight Omelets

Servings: 2

Cooking Time: 45 Minutes

Ingredients:

- 1 tablespoon unsalted butter, softened
- 2 slices hearty white sandwich bread
- 2 ounces cheddar cheese, shredded (½ cup)
- 3 large eggs
- ¾ cup whole milk

- 1 teaspoon minced fresh thyme or ¼ teaspoon dried
- ¼ teaspoon table salt
- ¼ teaspoon pepper

Directions:

1. Spray two 12-ounce ramekins with vegetable oil spray. Spread butter evenly over 1 side of bread slices, then cut into 1-inch pieces. Scatter half of bread evenly in prepared ramekins and sprinkle with half of cheddar. Repeat with remaining bread and cheese.

2. Whisk eggs, milk, thyme, salt, and pepper in bowl until well combined. Pour egg mixture evenly over bread and press lightly on bread to submerge. Wrap ramekins tightly with plastic wrap and refrigerate for at least 8 hours or up to 24 hours.

3. Adjust toaster oven rack to middle position and preheat the toaster oven to 350 degrees. Unwrap ramekins and place ramekins on small rimmed baking sheet. Bake until puffed and golden, 30 to 35 minutes, rotating sheet halfway through baking. Serve immediately.

Blueberry Muffins

Servings: 8

Cooking Time: 14 Minutes

Ingredients:

- 1⅓ cups flour
- ½ cup sugar
- 2 teaspoons baking powder
- ¼ teaspoon salt
- ⅓ cup canola oil

- 1 egg
- ½ cup milk
- ⅔ cup blueberries, fresh or frozen and thawed
- 8 foil muffin cups including paper liners

Directions:

1. Preheat the toaster oven to 330°F.

2. In a medium bowl, stir together flour, sugar, baking powder, and salt.

3. In a separate bowl, combine oil, egg, and milk and mix well.

4. Add egg mixture to dry ingredients and stir just until moistened.

5. Gently stir in blueberries.

6. Spoon batter evenly into muffin cups.

7. Place 4 muffin cups in air fryer oven and bake at 330°F for 14 minutes or until tops spring back when touched lightly.

8. Repeat previous step to cook remaining muffins.

Stromboli

Servings: 4

Cooking Time: 30 Minutes

Ingredients:

- CRUST
- 2 cups all-purpose flour
- 2 tablespoons unsalted butter, cut into small pieces
- 1 teaspoon table salt
- 2 teaspoons active dry yeast
- 2 teaspoons sugar
- TOPPINGS
- ½ cup marinara or pizza sauce

- ½ teaspoon Italian seasoning
- 2 ounces pepperoni slices
- 2 ounces salami slices
- 2 ounces thin ham slices
- 1 ½ cups shredded mozzarella cheese
- 3 tablespoons shredded Parmesan cheese
- 1 large egg
- ½ teaspoon granulated garlic
- 1 teaspoon sesame seeds

Directions:

1. Make the crust: Place the flour in a large bowl and create a well. Place ⅔ cup water, the butter, and salt in a small microwave-safe bowl and microwave on High (100 percent) power for 30 seconds or until warm. (The temperature of the mixture should not be above 110 ºF.) Pour the liquid into the well. Sprinkle the yeast and sugar over the water mixture and allow to stand for 5 minutes. Mix the flour mixture until a dough forms. Oil a medium bowl and place the dough in the bowl. Cover and let rise for 1 hour.

2. Preheat the toaster oven to 375 ºF. Line a 12 x 12-inch baking pan with parchment paper.

3. Flour a clean surface and roll the dough into a 15 x 13 ½-inch rectangle. Place the dough diagonally on the prepared pan. Spread the marinara sauce over the surface of the dough to within ½ inch of all four edges. Sprinkle with the Italian seasoning. Layer the pepperoni, salami, and ham slices on top of the marinara. Sprinkle with the cheeses. Roll up as tightly as possible and pinch the seams to make sure nothings seeps out.

4. Whisk the egg, 1 tablespoon of water, and the garlic in a small bowl. Brush the egg wash over the stromboli and sprinkle with the sesame seeds. Bake for 25 to 30 minutes or until golden brown.

Best-ever Cinnamon Rolls

Servings: 10

Cooking Time: 18 Minutes

Ingredients:

- 1 tablespoon unsalted butter, softened
- DOUGH
- ½ cup whole milk
- 2 tablespoons unsalted butter, softened
- 3 tablespoons granulated sugar
- ½ teaspoon table salt
- 1 large egg
- 1 ⅔ cups all-purpose flour, plus more for kneading and dusting
- 1 ¼ teaspoons instant yeast
- FILLING
- ⅔ cup packed dark brown sugar
- 1 tablespoon plus 1 teaspoon ground cinnamon
- Pinch table salt
- 3 tablespoons unsalted butter, melted
- GLAZE
- 1 ½ cups confectioners' sugar
- 1 to 2 tablespoon whole milk
- 1 tablespoon brewed coffee
- ½ teaspoon pure vanilla extract
- 1 tablespoon unsalted butter, melted

Directions:

1. Spread the 1 tablespoon softened butter generously on the sides and bottom of an 8-inch round baking pan.

2. Combine the milk, 2 tablespoons softened butter, sugar, and salt in a 4-cup glass measuring cup. Microwave on High (100 percent) power for 40 seconds or until warm (110°F). (All the butter may not melt.) Whisk in the egg.

3. Stir the flour and yeast in a large bowl. Add the liquid ingredients and stir until you have a soft dough. Flour your hands and a clean surface. Transfer the dough to the floured surface and form it into a ball. Add flour as necessary and knead by pressing the dough with the heel of your hands and turning and repeating. Add just enough flour to keep the dough from being sticky.

4. When the dough is smooth and springs back when you press it with you finger (after 3 to 5 minutes of kneading), place the dough ball into a large oiled bowl, cover with a tea towel, and let rise in a warm place for about an hour or until the dough has almost doubled in size.

5. Transfer the dough to a floured surface and roll into a 10 x 14-inch rectangle.

6. Make the filling: Combine the brown sugar, cinnamon, and salt in a small bowl. Using a pastry brush, brush the melted butter over the entire surface of the dough. Sprinkle the cinnamon-sugar mixture over the butter, using your fingers to lightly press the mixture into the dough. Starting with the longer side, roll up the dough to form a 14-inch cylinder. Gently cut the cylinder into 10 even rolls, using a serrated knife.

Place in the prepared pan, cut side up. Cover and let rise in a warm place for about 45 to 60 minutes or until doubled.

7. Preheat the toaster oven to 350°F. Bake for 16 to 18 minutes or until slightly brown on top. Remove from the oven and place on a wire rack.

8. Meanwhile, make the glaze: Whisk the confectioners' sugar, 1 tablespoon milk, the coffee, vanilla, and butter in a medium bowl. If needed, whisk in the additional milk to make the desired consistency. Drizzle over the warm rolls.

Cherries Jubilee

Servings: 4
Cooking Time: 10 Minutes

Ingredients:
- 1 15-ounce can cherries, pitted and drained, with 2 tablespoons juice reserved
- 1 tablespoon orange juice
- 1 tablespoon sugar
- 1 tablespoon cornstarch
- ¼ cup warmed Kirsch or Cognac
- Vanilla yogurt or fat-free half-and-half

Directions:
1. Combine the reserved juice, orange juice, sugar, and cornstarch in a shallow baking pan, blending well.

2. BROIL for 5 minutes, or until the juice clarifies and thickens slightly. Add the cherries and heat, broiling for 5 minutes more and stirring to blend. Remove from the oven and transfer to a flameproof serving dish.

3. Spoon the Kirsch over the cherries and ignite. Top with vanilla yogurt or drizzle with warm fat-free half-and-half and serve.

Cheddar Bacon Broiler

Servings: 4

Cooking Time: 8 Minutes

Ingredients:

- 4 slices pumpernickel bread
- 4 strips lean turkey bacon, cut in half
- 4 tablespoons shredded Cheddar cheese
- 4 tablespoons grated Parmesan cheese
- 4 tablespoons finely chopped bell pepper
- 1 medium tomato, chopped
- 2 tablespoons finely chopped onion
- Salt and freshly ground black pepper
- 2 tablespoons chopped fresh parsley or cilantro

Directions:

1. Layer the bread slices with 2 half strips turkey bacon and 1 tablespoon each Cheddar cheese, Parmesan cheese, and bell pepper. Sprinkle each with equal portions of tomato and onion. Season to taste with salt and pepper.

2. BROIL on a broiling rack with a pan underneath for 8 minutes, or until the cheese is well melted. Before serving, sprinkle with parsley or cilantro.

Lemon Blueberry Scones

Servings: 6

Cooking Time: 25 Minutes

Ingredients:

- 1 ½ cups all-purpose flour
- 2 tablespoons granulated sugar
- 2 ¼ teaspoons baking powder
- 1 teaspoon grated lemon zest
- ¼ teaspoon table salt
- ¼ cup unsalted butter, cut into 1-tablespoon pieces
- ¾ cup fresh or frozen blueberries
- ¾ cup plus 1 tablespoon heavy cream, plus more for brushing
- Coarse white sugar
- LEMON GLAZE
- 1 cup confectioners' sugar
- 2 to 3 tablespoons fresh lemon juice

Directions:

1. Line a 12 x 12-inch baking pan with parchment paper.

2. Whisk the flour, granulated sugar, baking powder, lemon zest, and salt in a large bowl. Cut in the butter using a pastry cutter or two knives until the mixture is crumbly throughout. Gently stir in the blueberries, taking care not to mash them. Add ¾ cup cream and gently stir until a soft dough forms. If needed, stir in an additional tablespoon of cream so all of the flour is moistened.

3. Turn the dough onto a lightly floured board. Pat the dough into a circle about ¾ inch thick and 6 inches in diameter. Cut into 6 triangles. Arrange the triangles on the prepared pan. Freeze for 15 minutes.

4. Preheat the toaster oven to 400°F. Brush the scones lightly with cream and sprinkle with coarse sugar. Bake for 20 to 25 minutes or until golden brown. Let cool for 5 minutes.

5. Meanwhile, make the glaze: Stir the confectioners' sugar and lemon juice in a small bowl, blending until smooth. Drizzle the glaze over the scones. Let stand for about 5 minutes. These taste best served freshly made and slightly warm.

Strawberry Pie

Servings: 6
Cooking Time: 25 Minutes

Ingredients:

- 2 16-ounce packages frozen sliced strawberries or 1 quart fresh strawberries, washed, stemmed, and sliced
- ¼ cup sugar
- 2 tablespoons lemon juice
- 2 tablespoons cornstarch
- 1 single Oatmeal Piecrust, baked (recipe follows)
- Strawberry Pie Glaze (recipe follows)

Directions:

1. Preheat the toaster oven to 350° F.
2. Combine the strawberries, sugar, lemon juice, and cornstarch in a medium bowl, mixing well. Fill the piecrust shell with the strawberries, spreading evenly.
3. BAKE for 25 minutes, or until the strawberries are tender. Glaze with Strawberry Pie Glaze.

Western Omelet

Servings: 2
Cooking Time: 22 Minutes

Ingredients:

- ¼ cup chopped onion
- ¼ cup chopped bell pepper, green or red
- ¼ cup diced ham
- 1 teaspoon butter
- 4 large eggs
- 2 tablespoons milk
- ⅛ teaspoon salt
- ¾ cup grated sharp Cheddar cheese

Directions:

1. Place onion, bell pepper, ham, and butter in air fryer oven baking pan. Air-fry at 390°F for 1 minute and stir. Continue cooking 5 minutes, until vegetables are tender.
2. Beat together eggs, milk, and salt. Pour over vegetables and ham in baking pan. Air-fry at 360°F for 15 minutes or until eggs set and top has browned slightly.
3. Sprinkle grated cheese on top of omelet. Cook 1 minute or just long enough to melt the cheese.

Bacon Cheddar Biscuits

Servings: 6
Cooking Time: 15 Minutes

Ingredients:

- 1 cup all-purpose flour
- 1 tablespoon baking powder
- ¼ teaspoon table salt
- ¼ teaspoon smoked paprika or freshly ground black pepper
- 3 tablespoons unsalted butter
- ½ cup whole milk

- 1 cup shredded sharp cheddar cheese
- 2 tablespoons minced fresh chives
- 4 slices bacon, cooked until crisp and crumbled

Directions:

1. Preheat the toaster oven to 425°F.

2. Stir the flour, baking powder, salt, and paprika in a large bowl. Using a pastry cutter or two knives, cut the butter into the flour mixture until the mixture is crumbly throughout. Pour in the milk and gently mix until just combined. Stir in the cheese, chives, and bacon.

3. Turn the dough onto a lightly floured surface and knead lightly about 8 times. Roll the dough, using a rolling pin, until about ¾ inch thick. Cut out rounds using a 2-inch cutter. Place 1 inch apart on an ungreased 12 x 12-inch baking pan. Bake for 12 to 15 minutes or until golden brown.

Espresso Chip Muffins

Servings: 6

Cooking Time: 20 Minutes

Ingredients:

- 1 cup all-purpose flour
- 6 tablespoons packed dark brown sugar
- 1 ¼ teaspoons baking powder
- 1 teaspoon instant espresso coffee powder
- ¼ teaspoon table salt
- ¼ teaspoon ground cinnamon
- ½ cup whole milk
- ¼ cup unsalted butter, melted and cooled slightly
- 1 large egg

- ½ teaspoon pure vanilla extract
- ½ cup mini semisweet chocolate chips

Directions:

1. Preheat the toaster oven to 375°F. Grease a 6-cup muffin pan.

2. Whisk the flour, brown sugar, baking powder, espresso, salt, and cinnamon in a medium bowl. Combine the milk, butter, egg, and vanilla in a small bowl until blended. Make a well in the center of the flour mixture and add the milk mixture. Stir until just combined. Fold in the chocolate chips.

3. Spoon the batter evenly into the prepared muffin cups. Bake for 18 to 20 minutes, or until a wooden pick inserted into the center comes out clean. Cool on a wire rack for 5 minutes, then remove the muffins from the pan to finish cooling on a wire rack. Serve warm or at room temperature. Store in an airtight container.

Cinnamon Sugar Donut Holes

Servings: 12

Cooking Time: 6 Minutes

Ingredients:

- 1 cup all-purpose flour
- 6 tablespoons cane sugar, divided
- 1 teaspoon baking powder
- 3 teaspoons ground cinnamon, divided
- ¼ teaspoon salt
- 1 large egg
- 1 teaspoon vanilla extract
- 2 tablespoons melted butter

Directions:

1. Preheat the toaster oven to 370°F.

2. In a small bowl, combine the flour, 2 tablespoons of the sugar, the baking powder, 1 teaspoon of the cinnamon, and the salt. Mix well.

3. In a larger bowl, whisk together the egg, vanilla extract, and butter.

4. Slowly add the dry ingredients into the wet until all the ingredients are uniformly combined. Set the bowl inside the refrigerator for at least 30 minutes.

5. Before you're ready to cook, in a small bowl, mix together the remaining 4 tablespoons of sugar and 2 teaspoons of cinnamon.

6. Liberally spray the air fryer oven with olive oil mist so the donut holes don't stick to the bottom.

7. Remove the dough from the refrigerator and divide it into 12 equal donut holes. You can use a 1-ounce serving scoop if you have one.

8. Roll each donut hole in the sugar and cinnamon mixture; then place in the air fryer oven. Repeat until all the donut holes are covered in the sugar and cinnamon mixture.

9. When the oven is full, air-fry for 6 minutes. Remove the donut holes from the oven using oven-safe tongs and let cool 5 minutes. Repeat until all 12 are cooked.

- 1 teaspoon ground cinnamon
- ⅛ teaspoon salt
- 1 large egg
- ⅓ cup packed brown sugar
- ¼ cup canola oil
- 1 teaspoon vanilla extract
- ⅓ cup milk
- 1 medium zucchini, shredded (about 1⅓ cups)
- ⅓ cup chopped walnuts

Directions:

1. Preheat the toaster oven to 320°F.

2. In a medium bowl, mix together the flour, baking soda, cinnamon, and salt.

3. In a large bowl, whisk together the egg, brown sugar, oil, vanilla, and milk. Stir in the zucchini.

4. Slowly fold the dry ingredients into the wet ingredients. Stir in the chopped walnuts. Then pour the batter into two 4-inch oven-safe loaf pans.

5. Bake for 30 minutes or until a toothpick inserted into the center comes out clean. Let cool before slicing.

6. Store tightly wrapped on the counter for up to 5 days, in the refrigerator for up to 10 days, or in the freezer for 3 months.

Zucchini Walnut Bread

Servings: 6

Cooking Time: 30 Minutes

Ingredients:

- ¾ cup all-purpose flour
- ½ teaspoon baking soda

Breakfast Pita

Servings: 2

Cooking Time: 3 Minutes

Ingredients:

- 1 5-inch whole wheat pita loaf
- 1 teaspoon olive oil

- 1 egg, well beaten
- 2 tablespoons shredded low-fat mozzarella cheese
- Garlic powder
- Salt and freshly ground black pepper

Directions:

1. Cut a circle out of the top layer of one pita bread loaf and remove the disk-shaped layer, leaving the bottom intact. Brush the pita loaf with the olive oil. Carefully pour the beaten egg into the cavity. Sprinkle with cheese and season with garlic powder and salt and pepper to taste.

2. TOAST once on the oven rack, or until the egg is cooked thoroughly and the cheese is lightly browned.

FISH AND SEAFOOD

Baked Clam Appetizers

Servings: 12

Cooking Time: 10 Minutes

Ingredients:

- 1 6-ounce can minced clams, well drained
- 1 cup multigrain bread crumbs
- 1 tablespoon minced onion
- 1 teaspoon garlic powder
- 1 teaspoon Worcestershire sauce
- 1 tablespoon chopped fresh parsley
- 2 tablespoons olive oil
- Salt and freshly ground black pepper
- Lemon wedges

Directions:

1. Preheat the toaster oven to 450° F.

2. Combine all the ingredients in a medium bowl and fill 12 scrubbed clamshells or small baking dishes with equal portions of the mixture. Place in an 8½ × 8½ × 2-inch oiled or nonstick square (cake) pan.

3. BAKE for 10 minutes, or until lightly browned.

Fish Tacos With Jalapeño-lime Sauce

Servings: 4

Cooking Time: 7 Minutes

Ingredients:

- Fish Tacos

- 1 pound fish fillets
- ¼ teaspoon cumin
- ¼ teaspoon coriander
- ⅛ teaspoon ground red pepper
- 1 tablespoon lime zest
- ¼ teaspoon smoked paprika
- 1 teaspoon oil
- cooking spray
- 6–8 corn or flour tortillas (6-inch size)
- Jalapeño-Lime Sauce
- ½ cup sour cream
- 1 tablespoon lime juice
- ¼ teaspoon grated lime zest
- ½ teaspoon minced jalapeño (flesh only)
- ¼ teaspoon cumin
- Napa Cabbage Garnish
- 1 cup shredded Napa cabbage
- ¼ cup slivered red or green bell pepper
- ¼ cup slivered onion

Directions:

1. Slice the fish fillets into strips approximately ½-inch thick.

2. Put the strips into a sealable plastic bag along with the cumin, coriander, red pepper, lime zest, smoked paprika, and oil. Massage seasonings into the fish until evenly distributed.

3. Spray air fryer oven with nonstick cooking spray and place seasoned fish inside.

4. Air-fry at 390°F for approximately 5 minutes. Distribute fish. Cook an additional 2 minutes, until fish flakes easily.

5. While the fish is cooking, prepare the Jalapeño-Lime Sauce by mixing the sour cream, lime juice, lime zest, jalapeño, and cumin together to make a smooth sauce. Set aside.

6. Mix the cabbage, bell pepper, and onion together and set aside.

7. To warm refrigerated tortillas, wrap in damp paper towels and microwave for 30 to 60 seconds.

8. To serve, spoon some of fish into a warm tortilla. Add one or two tablespoons Napa Cabbage Garnish and drizzle with Jalapeño-Lime Sauce.

Mediterranean Baked Fish

Servings: 4
Cooking Time: 25 Minutes

Ingredients:
- Baking mixture:
- 1 tablespoon olive oil
- 2 tablespoons tomato paste
- 3 plum tomatoes, chopped
- 2 garlic cloves, minced
- 2 tablespoons capers
- 2 tablespoons pitted and chopped black olives
- 2 tablespoons chopped fresh basil leaves
- 2 tablespoons chopped fresh parsley
- 4 6-ounce fish fillets (red snapper, cod, whiting, sole, or mackerel)

Directions:
1. Preheat the toaster oven to 350° F.
2. Combine the baking mixture ingredients in a small bowl. Set aside.

3. Layer the fillets in an oiled or nonstick 8½ × 8½ × 2-inch square baking (cake) pan, overlapping them if necessary, and spoon the baking mixture over the fish.

4. BAKE, covered, for 25 minutes, or until the fish flakes easily with a fork.

Almond Crab Cakes

Servings: 4
Cooking Time: 10 Minutes

Ingredients:
- 1 pound cooked lump crabmeat, drained and picked over
- ¼ cup ground almonds
- 1 tablespoon Dijon mustard
- 1 scallion, white and green parts, finely chopped
- ½ red bell pepper, finely chopped
- 1 large egg
- 1 teaspoon lemon zest
- Oil spray (hand-pumped)
- 3 tablespoons almond flour

Directions:
1. Preheat the toaster oven to 375°F on AIR FRY for 5 minutes.

2. In a medium bowl, mix the crab meat, almonds, mustard, scallion, bell pepper, egg, and lemon zest until well combined and the mixture holds together when pressed. If the crab cakes do not stick together, add more ground almond.

3. Divide the crab mixture into 8 patties and press them to about 1 inch thick. Place them on a plate, cover, and chill for 30 minutes.

4. Place the air-fryer basket in the baking tray and generously spray with the oil.

5. Place the almond flour on a plate and dredge the crab cakes until they are lightly coated.

6. Place them in the basket and lightly spray both sides with the oil.

7. In position 2, air fry for 10 minutes, turning halfway through, until golden brown. Serve.

Chilled Clam Cake Slices With Dijon Dill Sauce

Servings: 6
Cooking Time: 30 Minutes

Ingredients:
- 1 10-ounce can minced clams, drained
- 1 egg
- ¾ cup multigrain bread crumbs
- 1 tablespoon vegetable oil
- 1 cup skim milk
- ¼ cup chopped onions
- 2 tablespoons chopped pimientos, drained
- Salt and freshly ground black pepper to taste
- Dijon Dill Sauce (recipe follows)

Directions:
1. Preheat the toaster oven to 400° F.
2. Combine all the ingredients in a medium bowl, mixing well. Transfer to an 8½ × 8½ × 2-inch oiled or nonstick square (cake) pan.
3. BAKE for 30 minutes, or until the top is browned. Let cool, then chill the loaf in the refrigerator. Cut into thin slices or squares and serve with the sauce.

Roasted Pepper Tilapia

Servings: 6

Cooking Time: 20 Minutes

Ingredients:
- 6 5-ounce tilapia fillets
- 2 tablespoons olive oil
- Filling:
- 1 cucumber, peeled, seeds scooped out and discarded, and chopped
- ½ cup chopped roasted peppers, drained
- 2 tablespoons lemon juice
- 2 tablespoons chopped fresh parsley or cilantro
- 1 teaspoon garlic powder
- 1 teaspoon paprika
- Salt and freshly ground black pepper to taste
- Dip mixture:
- 1 cup nonfat sour cream
- 2 tablespoons low-fat mayonnaise
- 3 tablespoons Dijon mustard
- 1 teaspoon Worcestershire sauce
- 1 teaspoon dried dill

Directions:
1. Combine the filling ingredients in a bowl, adjusting the seasonings to taste.
2. Spoon equal portions of filling in the centers of the tilapia filets. Roll up the fillets, starting at the smallest end. Secure each roll with toothpicks and place the rolls in an oiled or nonstick baking pan. Carefully brush the fillets with oil and place them in an oiled or nonstick 8½ × 8½ × 2-inch square baking (cake) pan.
3. BROIL for 20 minutes, or until the fillets are lightly browned. Combine the dip mixture ingredients in a small bowl and serve with the fish.

Crunchy And Buttery Cod With Ritz® Cracker Crust

Servings: 2

Cooking Time: 10 Minutes

Ingredients:

- 4 tablespoons butter, melted
- 8 to 10 RITZ® crackers, crushed into crumbs
- 2 (6-ounce) cod fillets
- salt and freshly ground black pepper
- 1 lemon

Directions:

1. Preheat the toaster oven to 380°F.

2. Melt the butter in a small saucepan on the stovetop or in a microwavable dish in the microwave, and then transfer the butter to a shallow dish. Place the crushed RITZ® crackers into a second shallow dish.

3. Season the fish fillets with salt and freshly ground black pepper. Dip them into the butter and then coat both sides with the RITZ® crackers.

4. Place the fish into the air fryer oven and air-fry at 380°F for 10 minutes, flipping the fish over halfway through the cooking time.

5. Serve with a wedge of lemon to squeeze over the top.

Flounder Fillets

Servings: 4

Cooking Time: 8 Minutes

Ingredients:

- 1 egg white
- 1 tablespoon water
- 1 cup panko breadcrumbs
- 2 tablespoons extra-light virgin olive oil
- 4 4-ounce flounder fillets
- salt and pepper
- oil for misting or cooking spray

Directions:

1. Preheat the toaster oven to 390°F.

2. Beat together egg white and water in shallow dish.

3. In another shallow dish, mix panko crumbs and oil until well combined and crumbly (best done by hand).

4. Season flounder fillets with salt and pepper to taste. Dip each fillet into egg mixture and then roll in panko crumbs, pressing in crumbs so that fish is nicely coated.

5. Spray air fryer oven with nonstick cooking spray and add fillets. Air-fry at 390°F for 3 minutes.

6. Spray fish fillets but do not turn. Cook 5 minutes longer or until golden brown and crispy. Using a spatula, carefully remove fish from air fryer oven and serve.

Pecan-crusted Tilapia

Servings: 4

Cooking Time: 8 Minutes

Ingredients:

- 1 pound skinless, boneless tilapia filets
- ¼ cup butter, melted
- 1 teaspoon minced fresh or dried rosemary
- 1 cup finely chopped pecans
- 1 teaspoon sea salt

- ¼ teaspoon paprika
- 2 tablespoons chopped parsley
- 1 lemon, cut into wedges

Directions:

1. Pat the tilapia filets dry with paper towels.

2. Pour the melted butter over the filets and flip the filets to coat them completely.

3. In a medium bowl, mix together the rosemary, pecans, salt, and paprika.

4. Preheat the toaster oven to 350°F.

5. Place the tilapia filets into the air fryer oven and top with the pecan coating. Air-fry for 6 to 8 minutes. The fish should be firm to the touch and flake easily when fully cooked.

6. Remove the fish from the air fryer oven. Top the fish with chopped parsley and serve with lemon wedges.

Maple-crusted Salmon

Servings: 2

Cooking Time: 8 Minutes

Ingredients:

- 12 ounces salmon filets
- ⅓ cup maple syrup
- 1 teaspoon Worcestershire sauce
- 2 teaspoons Dijon mustard or brown mustard
- ½ cup finely chopped walnuts
- ½ teaspoon sea salt
- ½ lemon
- 1 tablespoon chopped parsley, for garnish

Directions:

1. Place the salmon in a shallow baking dish. Top with maple syrup, Worcestershire sauce, and mustard. Refrigerate for 30 minutes.

2. Preheat the toaster oven to 350°F.

3. Remove the salmon from the marinade and discard the marinade.

4. Place the chopped nuts on top of the salmon filets, and sprinkle salt on top of the nuts. Place the salmon, skin side down, in the air fryer oven. Air-fry for 6 to 8 minutes or until the fish flakes in the center.

5. Remove the salmon and plate on a serving platter. Squeeze fresh lemon over the top of the salmon and top with chopped parsley. Serve immediately.

Tuna Nuggets In Hoisin Sauce

Servings: 4

Cooking Time: 7 Minutes

Ingredients:

- ½ cup hoisin sauce
- 2 tablespoons rice wine vinegar
- 2 teaspoons sesame oil
- 1 teaspoon garlic powder
- 2 teaspoons dried lemongrass
- ¼ teaspoon red pepper flakes
- ½ small onion, quartered and thinly sliced
- 8 ounces fresh tuna, cut into 1-inch cubes
- cooking spray
- 3 cups cooked jasmine rice

Directions:

1. Mix the hoisin sauce, vinegar, sesame oil, and seasonings together.

2. Stir in the onions and tuna nuggets.

3. Spray air fryer oven baking pan with nonstick spray and pour in tuna mixture.

4. Air-fry at 390°F for 3 minutes. Stir gently.

5. Cook 2 minutes and stir again, checking for doneness. Tuna should be barely cooked through, just beginning to flake and still very moist. If necessary, continue cooking and stirring in 1-minute intervals until done.

6. Serve warm over hot jasmine rice.

Fish Sticks For Kids

Servings: 8

Cooking Time: 6 Minutes

Ingredients:

- 8 ounces fish fillets (pollock or cod)
- salt (optional)
- ½ cup plain breadcrumbs
- oil for misting or cooking spray

Directions:

1. Cut fish fillets into "fingers" about ½ x 3 inches. Sprinkle with salt to taste, if desired.

2. Roll fish in breadcrumbs. Spray all sides with oil or cooking spray.

3. Place in air fryer oven in single layer and air-fry at 390°F for 6 minutes, until golden brown and crispy.

Shrimp & Grits

Servings: 4

Cooking Time: 5 Minutes

Ingredients:

- 1 pound raw shelled shrimp, deveined (26–30 count or smaller)
- Marinade
- 2 tablespoons lemon juice
- 2 tablespoons Worcestershire sauce
- 1 tablespoon olive oil
- 1 teaspoon Old Bay Seasoning
- ½ teaspoon hot sauce
- Grits
- ¾ cup quick cooking grits (not instant)
- 3 cups water
- ½ teaspoon salt
- 1 tablespoon butter
- ½ cup chopped green bell pepper
- ½ cup chopped celery
- ½ cup chopped onion
- ½ teaspoon oregano
- ¼ teaspoon Old Bay Seasoning
- 2 ounces sharp Cheddar cheese, grated

Directions:

1. Stir together all marinade ingredients. Pour marinade over shrimp and set aside.

2. For grits, heat water and salt to boil in saucepan on stovetop. Stir in grits, lower heat to medium-low, and cook about 5 minutes or until thick and done.

3. Place butter, bell pepper, celery, and onion in air fryer oven baking pan. Air-fry at 390°F for 2 minutes and stir. Cook 6 or 7 minutes longer, until crisp tender.

4. Add oregano and 1 teaspoon Old Bay to cooked vegetables. Stir in grits and cheese and

air-fry at 390°F for 1 minute. Stir and cook 1 to 2 minutes longer to melt cheese.

5. Remove baking pan from air fryer oven. Cover with plate to keep warm while shrimp cooks.

6. Drain marinade from shrimp. Place shrimp in air fryer oven and air-fry at 360°F for 3 minutes. Cook 2 more minutes, until done.

7. To serve, spoon grits onto plates and top with shrimp.

Tasty Fillets With Poblano Sauce

Servings: 2
Cooking Time: 20 Minutes

Ingredients:

- 4 5-ounce thin fish fillets—perch, scrod, catfish, or flounder
- 1 tablespoon olive oil
- Poblano sauce:
- 1 poblano chili, seeded and chopped
- 1 bell pepper, seeded and chopped
- 2 tablespoons chopped onion
- 5 garlic cloves, peeled
- 1 tablespoon flour
- 1 cup fat-free half-and-half
- Salt to taste

Directions:

1. Preheat the toaster oven to 350° F.

2. Brush the fillets with olive oil and transfer to an oiled or nonstick 8½ × 8½ × 2-inch square baking (cake) pan. Set aside.

3. Combine the poblano sauce ingredients and process in a blender or food processor until smooth. Spoon the poblano sauce over the fillets, covering them well.

4. BAKE, uncovered, for 20 minutes, or until the fish flakes easily with a fork.

Romaine Wraps With Shrimp Filling

Servings: 4
Cooking Time: 8 Minutes

Ingredients:

- Filling:
- 1 6-ounce can tiny shrimp, drained, or 1 cup fresh shrimp, peeled, cooked, and chopped
- ¾ cup canned chickpeas, mashed into 1 tablespoon olive oil
- 2 tablespoons chopped fresh parsley
- 2 tablespoons grated carrot
- 2 tablespoons chopped bell pepper
- 2 tablespoons minced onion
- 2 tablespoons lemon juice
- 1 teaspoon soy sauce
- Freshly ground black pepper to taste
- 4 large romaine lettuce leaves Olive oil
- 3 tablespoons lemon juice
- 1 teaspoon paprika

Directions:

1. Combine the filling ingredients in a bowl, adjusting the seasonings to taste. Spoon equal portions of the filling into the centers of the romaine leaves. Fold the leaves in half, pressing the filling together, overlap the leaf edges, and skewer with toothpicks to fasten. Carefully place the leaves in an oiled or nonstick 8½ × 8½ × 2-

inch square baking (cake) pan. Lightly spray or brush the lettuce rolls with olive oil.

2. BROIL for 8 minutes, or until the filling is cooked and the leaves are lightly browned. Remove from the oven, remove the toothpicks, and drizzle with the lemon juice and sprinkle with paprika.

Spiced Sea Bass

Servings: 4
Cooking Time: 25 Minutes

Ingredients:

- Brushing mixture:
- 2 tablespoons lemon juice
- 1 tablespoon chopped fresh parsley
- 2 garlic cloves, minced
- 2 6-ounce sea bass fillets, approximately 1 inch thick
- Spice mixture:
- 2 teaspoons paprika
- 2 teaspoons ground cumin
- 1 teaspoon allspice
- 2 teaspoons garlic powder
- Pinch of cayenne
- Salt to taste

Directions:

1. Combine the brushing mixture ingredients in a small bowl, mixing well. Place the fillets on a plate or platter.

2. Brush the fillets on both sides with the brushing mixture. Let stand at room temperature for 10 minutes.

3. Combine the spice mixture ingredients in a small bowl, mixing well. Transfer to a plate and press the fillets into the spice mixture to coat well. Transfer the fillets to an oiled or nonstick 8½ × 8½ × 2-inch square baking (cake) pan.

4. BROIL for 15 minutes, or until the fish flakes easily with a fork.

Lemon-dill Salmon Burgers

Servings: 4
Cooking Time: 8 Minutes

Ingredients:

- 2 (6-ounce) fillets of salmon, finely chopped by hand or in a food processor
- 1 cup fine breadcrumbs
- 1 teaspoon freshly grated lemon zest
- 2 tablespoons chopped fresh dill weed
- 1 teaspoon salt
- freshly ground black pepper
- 2 eggs, lightly beaten
- 4 brioche or hamburger buns
- lettuce, tomato, red onion, avocado, mayonnaise or mustard, to serve

Directions:

1. Preheat the toaster oven to 400°F.

2. Combine all the ingredients in a bowl. Mix together well and divide into four balls. Flatten the balls into patties, making an indentation in the center of each patty with your thumb (this will help the burger stay flat as it cooks) and flattening the sides of the burgers so that they fit nicely into the air fryer oven.

3. Transfer the burgers to the air fryer oven and air-fry for 4 minutes. Flip the burgers over and air-fry for another 3 to 4 minutes, until nicely browned and firm to the touch.

4. Serve on soft brioche buns with your choice of topping – lettuce, tomato, red onion, avocado, mayonnaise or mustard.

Shrimp Po'boy With Remoulade Sauce

Servings: 6

Cooking Time: 8 Minutes

Ingredients:

- ½ cup all-purpose flour
- ½ teaspoon paprika
- 1 teaspoon garlic powder
- ½ teaspoon black pepper
- ¼ teaspoon salt
- 2 eggs, whisked
- 1½ cups panko breadcrumbs
- 1 pound small shrimp, peeled and deveined
- Six 6-inch French rolls
- 2 cups shredded lettuce
- 12 ⅛-inch tomato slices
- ¾ cup Remoulade Sauce (see the following recipe)

Directions:

1. Preheat the toaster oven to 360°F.

2. In a medium bowl, mix the flour, paprika, garlic powder, pepper, and salt.

3. In a shallow dish, place the eggs.

4. In a third dish, place the panko breadcrumbs.

5. Covering the shrimp in the flour, dip them into the egg, and coat them with the breadcrumbs. Repeat until all shrimp are covered in the breading.

6. Liberally spray the metal trivet that fits inside the air fryer oven with olive oil spray. Place the shrimp onto the trivet, leaving space between the shrimp to flip. Air-fry for 4 minutes, flip the shrimp, and cook another 4 minutes. Repeat until all the shrimp are cooked.

7. Slice the rolls in half. Stuff each roll with shredded lettuce, tomato slices, breaded shrimp, and remoulade sauce. Serve immediately.

Lemon-roasted Fish With Olives + Capers

Servings: 4

Cooking Time: 10 Minutes

Ingredients:

- Nonstick cooking spray
- 1 pound cod or white-fleshed, mild-flavored fillets, patted dry
- Kosher salt and freshly ground black pepper
- ½ teaspoon paprika
- 1 large lemon
- 3 tablespoons dry white wine
- ½ cup pitted kalamata or other variety olives, drained
- 2 tablespoons capers, drained
- 1 tablespoon olive oil

Directions:

1. Preheat the toaster oven to 425°F. Spray a 12 x 12-inch baking pan with nonstick cooking spray.

2. Place the fish fillets on the prepared pan. Season with salt, pepper, and paprika.

3. Slice the lemon in half. Slice one half crosswise into almost paper-thin slices. Arrange the slices evenly over the fish. Juice the remaining half of the lemon and drizzle over the fish. Drizzle the wine over the fish. Top with the olives and capers, then drizzle with the olive oil.

4. Roast for 10 minutes or until the fish flakes easily with a fork and a meat thermometer registers 145°F. To serve, spoon the pan drippings, olives, and capers over the fish.

Bacon-wrapped Scallops

Servings: 4

Cooking Time: 8 Minutes

Ingredients:

- 16 large scallops
- 8 bacon strips
- ½ teaspoon black pepper
- ¼ teaspoon smoked paprika

Directions:

1. Pat the scallops dry with a paper towel. Slice each of the bacon strips in half. Wrap 1 bacon strip around 1 scallop and secure with a toothpick. Repeat with the remaining scallops. Season the scallops with pepper and paprika.

2. Preheat the toaster oven to 350°F.

3. Place the bacon-wrapped scallops in the air fryer oven and air-fry for 4 minutes. Cook another 6 to 7 minutes. When the bacon is crispy, the scallops should be cooked through and slightly firm, but not rubbery. Serve immediately.

Snapper With Capers And Olives

Servings: 2

Cooking Time: 10 Minutes

Ingredients:

- 2 tablespoons capers
- ¼ cup pitted and sliced black olives
- 2 tablespoons olive oil
- ½ teaspoon dried oregano
- Salt and freshly ground black pepper to taste
- 2 6-ounce red snapper fillets
- 1 tomato, cut into wedges

Directions:

1. Combine the capers, olives, olive oil, and seasonings in a bowl.

2. Place the fillets in an oiled or nonstick 8½ × 8½ × 2-inch square baking (cake) pan and spoon the caper mixture over them.

3. BROIL for 10 minutes, or until the fish flakes easily with a fork. Serve with the tomato wedges.

Sesame-crusted Tuna Steaks

Servings: 3

Cooking Time: 13 Minutes

Ingredients:

- ½ cup Sesame seeds, preferably a blend of white and black
- 1½ tablespoons Toasted sesame oil
- 3 6-ounce skinless tuna steaks

Directions:

1. Preheat the toaster oven to 400°F.

2. Pour the sesame seeds on a dinner plate. Use ½ tablespoon of the sesame oil as a rub on both

sides and the edges of a tuna steak. Set it in the sesame seeds, then turn it several times, pressing gently, to create an even coating of the seeds, including around the steak's edge. Set aside and continue coating the remaining steak(s).

3. When the machine is at temperature, set the steaks in the air fryer oven with as much air space between them as possible. Air-fry undisturbed for 10 minutes for medium-rare (not USDA-approved), or 12 to 13 minutes for cooked through (USDA-approved).

4. Use a nonstick-safe spatula to transfer the steaks to serving plates. Serve hot.

Spicy Fish Street Tacos With Sriracha Slaw

Servings: 2

Cooking Time: 5 Minutes

Ingredients:

- Sriracha Slaw:
- ½ cup mayonnaise
- 2 tablespoons rice vinegar
- 1 teaspoon sugar
- 2 tablespoons sriracha chili sauce
- 5 cups shredded green cabbage
- ¼ cup shredded carrots
- 2 scallions, chopped
- salt and freshly ground black pepper
- Tacos:
- ½ cup flour
- 1 teaspoon chili powder
- ½ teaspoon ground cumin
- 1 teaspoon salt
- freshly ground black pepper
- ½ teaspoon baking powder
- 1 egg, beaten
- ¼ cup milk
- 1 cup breadcrumbs
- 1 pound mahi-mahi or snapper fillets
- 1 tablespoon canola or vegetable oil
- 6 (6-inch) flour tortillas
- 1 lime, cut into wedges

Directions:

1. Start by making the sriracha slaw. Combine the mayonnaise, rice vinegar, sugar, and sriracha sauce in a large bowl. Mix well and add the green cabbage, carrots, and scallions. Toss until all the vegetables are coated with the dressing and season with salt and pepper. Refrigerate the slaw until you are ready to serve the tacos.

2. Combine the flour, chili powder, cumin, salt, pepper and baking powder in a bowl. Add the egg and milk and mix until the batter is smooth. Place the breadcrumbs in shallow dish.

3. Cut the fish fillets into 1-inch wide sticks, approximately 4-inches long. You should have about 12 fish sticks total. Dip the fish sticks into the batter, coating all sides. Let the excess batter drip off the fish and then roll them in the breadcrumbs, patting the crumbs onto all sides of the fish sticks. Set the coated fish on a plate or baking sheet until all the fish has been coated.

4. Preheat the toaster oven to 400°F.

5. Spray the coated fish sticks with oil on all sides. Spray or brush the inside of the air fryer oven with oil and transfer the fish to the air fryer

oven. Place as many sticks as you can in one layer, leaving a little room around each stick. Place any remaining sticks on top, perpendicular to the first layer.

6. Air-fry the fish for 3 minutes. Turn the fish sticks over and air-fry for an additional 2 minutes.

7. While the fish is air-frying, warm the tortilla shells either in a 350°F oven wrapped in foil or in a skillet with a little oil over medium-high heat for a couple minutes. Fold the tortillas in half and keep them warm until the remaining tortillas and fish are ready.

8. To assemble the tacos, place two pieces of the fish in each tortilla shell and top with the sriracha slaw. Squeeze the lime wedge over top and dig in.

Shrimp

Servings: 4
Cooking Time: 8 Minutes

Ingredients:

- 1 pound (26–30 count) shrimp, peeled, deveined, and butterflied (last tail section of shell intact)
- Marinade
- 1 5-ounce can evaporated milk
- 2 eggs, beaten
- 2 tablespoons white vinegar
- 1 tablespoon baking powder
- Coating
- 1 cup crushed panko breadcrumbs
- ½ teaspoon paprika
- ½ teaspoon Old Bay Seasoning
- ¼ teaspoon garlic powder

- oil for misting or cooking spray

Directions:

1. Stir together all marinade ingredients until well mixed. Add shrimp and stir to coat. Refrigerate for 1 hour.

2. When ready to cook, preheat the toaster oven to 390°F.

3. Combine coating ingredients in shallow dish.

4. Remove shrimp from marinade, roll in crumb mixture, and spray with olive oil or cooking spray.

5. Cooking in two batches, place shrimp in air fryer oven in single layer, close but not overlapping. Air-fry at 390°F for 8 minutes, until light golden brown and crispy.

6. Repeat step 5 to cook remaining shrimp.

Crab Cakes

Servings: 4
Cooking Time: 9 Minutes

Ingredients:

- 1 pound lump crab meat, checked for shells
- ⅓ cup breadcrumbs
- ¼ cup finely chopped onions
- ¼ cup finely chopped red bell peppers
- ¼ cup finely chopped parsley
- ¼ teaspoon sea salt
- 2 eggs, whisked
- ¾ cup mayonnaise, divided
- ¼ cup sour cream
- 1 lemon, divided
- ¼ cup sweet pickle relish
- 1 tablespoon prepared mustard

Directions:

1. In a large bowl, mix together the crab meat, breadcrumbs, onions, bell peppers, parsley, sea salt, eggs, and ¼ cup of the mayonnaise.

2. Preheat the toaster oven to 380°F.

3. Form 8 patties with the crab cake mixture. Line the air fryer oven with parchment paper and place the crab cakes on the parchment paper. Spray with cooking spray. Air-fry for 4 minutes, turn over the crab cakes, spray with cooking spray, and air-fry for an additional 3 to 5 minutes, or until golden brown and the edges are crispy. Cook in batches as needed.

4. Meanwhile, make the sauce. In a small bowl, mix together the remaining ½ cup of mayonnaise, the sour cream, the juice from ½ of the lemon, the pickle relish, and the mustard.

5. Place the cooked crab cakes on a serving platter and serve with the remaining ½ lemon cut into wedges and the dipping sauce.

LUNCH AND DINNER

Chicken Noodle Soup

Servings: 4

Cooking Time: 45 Minutes

Ingredients:

- 1 cup egg noodles, uncooked
- 1 skinless, boneless chicken breast filet, cut into 1-inch pieces
- 1 carrot, peeled and chopped
- 1 celery stalk, chopped
- 1 plum tomato, chopped
- 1 small onion, peeled and chopped
- 1 tablespoon chopped fresh parsley
- 1 teaspoon dried basil
- Salt and freshly ground black pepper to taste

Directions:

1. Preheat the toaster oven to 400° F.

2. Combine all the ingredients with 3 cups water in a 1-quart 8½ × 8½ × 4-inch ovenproof baking dish.

3. BAKE, covered, for 45 minutes, or until the vegetables and chicken are tender.

Light Beef Stroganoff

Servings: 4

Cooking Time: 40 Minutes

Ingredients:

- Sauce:
- 1 cup skim milk
- 1 cup fat-free half-and-half
- 2 tablespoons reduced-fat cream cheese, at room temperature
- 4 tablespoons unbleached flour
- 2 pounds lean round or sirloin steak, cut into strips 2 inches long and ½ inch thick
- Browning mixture:
- 1 tablespoon soy sauce
- 2 tablespoons spicy brown mustard
- 1 tablespoon olive oil
- 2 teaspoons garlic powder
- Salt and freshly ground black pepper to taste

Directions:

1. Whisk together the sauce ingredients in a medium bowl until smooth. Set aside.

2. Combine the beef strips and browning mixture ingredients in an oiled or nonstick 8½ × 8½ × 2-inch square baking (cake) pan.

3. BROIL for 8 minutes, or until the strips are browned, turning with tongs after 4 minutes. Transfer to a 1-quart 8½ × 8½ × 4-inch ovenproof baking dish. Add the sauce and mix well. Adjust the seasonings to taste. Cover with aluminum foil.

4. BAKE, covered, for 40 minutes, or until the meat is tender.

Baked French Toast With Maple Bourbon Syrup

Servings: 6

Cooking Time: 40 Minutes

Ingredients:

- Nonstick cooking spray
- 4 tablespoons unsalted butter, melted
- ½ cup packed dark brown sugar
- ⅔ cup chopped pecans, toasted
- 6 (1-inch-thick) slices crusty artisan, brioche, or firm country bread
- 3 large eggs
- 1 cup milk
- 1 teaspoon pure vanilla extract
- ⅓ cup maple syrup
- 2 tablespoons bourbon

Directions:

1. Spray an 11 x 7 x 2 ½-inch baking dish with nonstick cooking spray. Pour the butter into the dish. Stir in the brown sugar and pecans. Arrange the bread at an angle in the dish, overlapping the bottom of the slices as necessary.

2. Whisk the eggs, milk, and vanilla in a medium bowl. Drizzle the milk mixture over the bread, taking care to pour slowly and moisten the edges of the bread. Cover and refrigerate overnight.

3. When ready to bake, preheat the toaster oven to 350°F. Bake, uncovered, for 30 to 35 minutes or until golden and set.

4. Mix the maple syrup and bourbon in a small bowl. Drizzle the syrup over the French toast.

Bake for 3 to 5 minutes. Let stand for 2 to 3 minutes, then serve warm.

Fillets En Casserole

Servings: 4

Cooking Time: 20 Minutes

Ingredients:

- ½ cup multigrain bread crumbs
- 4 6-ounce fish fillets
- Sauce:
- 2 tablespoons white wine
- 1 teaspoon Worcestershire sauce
- 1 teaspoon lemon juice
- 1 tablespoon vegetable oil
- 1 teaspoon Dijon mustard
- Salt and freshly ground black pepper to taste
- 2 tablespoons capers

Directions:

1. Preheat the toaster oven to 400° F.

2. Layer the bottom of an oiled or nonstick 8½ × 8½ × 2-inch square baking (cake) pan with the bread crumbs and place the fillets on the crumbs.

3. Combine the sauce ingredients, mixing well, and spoon over the fillets. Sprinkle with the capers.

4. BAKE, covered, for 20 minutes, or until the fish flakes easily with a fork.

Roasted Vegetable Gazpacho

Servings: 4

Cooking Time: 35 Minutes

Ingredients:

- Vegetables and seasonings:

- 1 bell pepper, thinly sliced
- ½ cup chopped celery
- ½ cup frozen or canned corn
- 1 medium onion, thinly sliced
- 1 small yellow squash, cut into 1-inch slices
- 1 small zucchini, cut into 1-inch slices
- 3 garlic cloves, chopped
- ½ teaspoon ground cumin
- 2 tablespoons olive oil
- Salt and freshly ground black pepper to taste
- 1 quart tomato juice
- 1 tablespoon lemon juice
- 3 tablespoons chopped fresh cilantro

Directions:

1. Preheat the toaster oven to 400°F.

2. Combine the vegetables and seasonings in an oiled or nonstick 8½ × 8½ × 2-inch square baking (cake) pan, mixing well.

3. BAKE, covered, for 25 minutes, or until the onions and celery are tender. Remove from the oven, uncover, and turn the vegetable pieces with tongs.

4. BROIL for 10 minutes, or until the vegetables are lightly browned. Remove from the oven and cool. Transfer to a large nonaluminum container and add the tomato juice, lemon juice, and cilantro. Adjust the seasonings.

5. Chill, covered, for several hours, preferably a day or two to enrich the flavor of the stock.

Italian Stuffed Zucchini Boats

Servings: 6
Cooking Time: 26 Minutes

Ingredients:

- 6 small zucchini, halved lengthwise
- 1 pound bulk hot sausage
- 1 small onion, chopped
- 2 cloves garlic, minced
- 1 small Roma tomato, seeded and chopped
- 1/4 cup Parmesan cheese
- 3 tablespoons tomato paste
- 2 teaspoons dried Italian seasoning
- 1 teaspoon salt
- 1/2 teaspoon coarse black pepper
- 1 cup shredded mozzarella cheese
- Sliced fresh basil

Directions:

1. Preheat the toaster oven to 350°F. Spray a 13x9-inch baking pan with nonstick cooking spray.

2. Scoop out center of zucchini halves. Reserve 1 1/2 cups. Place zucchini boats in baking pan.

3. In a large skillet over medium-high heat, cook sausage, stirring to crumble, about 6 minutes or until browned. Remove sausage to a medium bowl.

4. Add onion and garlic to skillet, cook until onion is translucent. Stir in reserved zucchini, sausage, tomatoes, Parmesan cheese, tomato paste, Italian seasoning, salt and black pepper.

5. Spoon mixture into the zucchini boats.

6. Bake for 20 minutes. Remove from oven and top with mozzarella cheese.

7. Bake an additional 5 to 6 minutes or until cheese is melted.

8. Sprinkle with sliced fresh basil before serving.

Connecticut Garden Chowder

Servings: 4

Cooking Time: 60 Minutes

Ingredients:

- Soup:
- ½ cup peeled and shredded potato
- ½ cup shredded carrot
- ½ cup shredded celery 2 plum tomatoes, chopped
- 1 small zucchini, shredded
- 2 bay leaves
- ¼ teaspoon sage
- 1 teaspoon garlic powder
- Salt and butcher's pepper to taste
- Chowder base:
- 2 tablespoons reduced-fat cream cheese, at room temperature
- ½ cup fat-free half-and-half
- 2 tablespoons unbleached flour
- 2 tablespoons chopped fresh parsley

Directions:

1. Preheat the toaster oven to 375° F.

2. Combine the soup ingredients in a 1-quart 8½ × 8½ × 4-inch ovenproof baking dish, mixing well. Adjust the seasonings to taste.

3. BAKE, covered, for 40 minutes, or until the vegetables are tender.

4. Whisk the chowder mixture ingredients together until smooth. Add the mixture to the cooked soup ingredients and stir well to blend.

5. BAKE, uncovered for 20 minutes, or until the stock is thickened. Ladle the soup into individual soup bowls and garnish with the parsley.

Chicken Gumbo

Servings: 4

Cooking Time: 40 Minutes

Ingredients:

- 2 skinless, boneless chicken breast halves, cut into 1-inch cubes
- ½ cup dry red wine
- 1 small onion, finely chopped
- 1 celery stalk, finely chopped
- 2 plum tomatoes, chopped
- 3 1 bell pepper, chopped
- 1 tablespoon minced fresh garlic
- 2 okra pods, stemmed, seeded, and finely chopped 1 bay leaf
- ½ teaspoon hot sauce
- ½ teaspoon dried thyme
- Salt and freshly ground black pepper to taste

Directions:

1. Preheat the toaster oven to 400° F.

2. Combine all the ingredients in a 1-quart 8½ × 8½ × 4-inch ovenproof baking dish. Adjust the seasonings to taste. Cover with aluminum foil.

3. BAKE, covered, for 40 minutes, or until the onion, pepper, and celery are tender. Discard the bay leaf before serving.

Individual Chicken Pot Pies

Servings: 4

Cooking Time: 25 Minutes

Ingredients:

- 3 tablespoons unsalted butter
- ½ medium onion, chopped

- 1 carrot, chopped
- 1 stalk celery, chopped
- 1 ¼ cups sliced button or white mushrooms
- 2 tablespoons all-purpose flour
- 1 ¼ cups whole milk
- 1 tablespoon fresh lemon juice
- ½ teaspoon dried thyme leaves
- Kosher salt and freshly ground black pepper
- 1 ½ cups chopped cooked chicken
- ½ cup frozen peas
- Nonstick cooking spray
- 1 sheet frozen puff pastry, about 9 inches square, thawed (½ of a 17.3-ounce package)
- 1 large egg

Directions:

1. Melt the butter in a large skillet over medium-high heat. Add the onion, carrot, and celery and cook, stirring frequently, for 3 minutes. Add the mushrooms and cook, stirring frequently, for 7 to 10 minutes or until the liquid has evaporated. Blend in the flour and cook, stirring for 1 minute. (Be sure all of the flour is blended into the butter and vegetables.) Gradually stir in the milk. Cook, stirring constantly, until the mixture bubbles and thickens. Stir in the lemon juice and thyme and season with salt and pepper. Stir in the chicken and peas. Remove from the heat and set aside.

2. Preheat the toaster oven to 375°F. Spray 4 (8-ounce) oven-safe ramekins with nonstick cooking spray.

3. Roll the puff pastry out on a lightly floured board, to make an even 10-inch square. Cut the pastry into circles using a 4-inch cutter.

4. Spoon a heaping ¾ cup of filling into each prepared ramekin. Place a puff pastry circle on top of each and crimp the edges to seal to the ramekin. Using the tip of a paring knife, cut 3 slits in each crust to allow steam to escape. Whisk the egg with 1 tablespoon water in a small bowl. Brush the egg mixture over the top of the crust.

5. Bake for 20 to 25 minutes, or until the crust is golden brown. Remove from the oven and let stand for 5 minutes before serving.

Slow Cooker Chicken Philly Cheesesteak Sandwich

Servings: 4

Cooking Time: 2 Minutes

Ingredients:

- 1 3/4 to 2 pounds chicken tenders
- 2 large green peppers, cut in strips
- 2 medium onions, sliced
- 1 1/2 tablespoons rotisserie seasoning
- 1/2 teaspoon salt
- 4 tablespoons Italian salad dressing
- 4 hoagie rolls, split
- 4 slices Cheddar or American cheese
- 1/4 cup banana pepper rings, optional
- Hot Sauce or ketchup, optional

Directions:

1. In slow cooker crock, combine chicken tenders, pepper strips and onion slices with rotisserie seasoning and salt.

2. Cook on HIGH for 2 to 2 1/2 hours or LOW for 4 to 5 hours.

3. Preheat the toaster oven broiler. Open rolls and place on a cookie sheet

4. Slice chicken tenders. Place back in slow cooker. With a slotted spoon, divide chicken, peppers and onions among rolls and drizzle with Italian dressing. Top with cheese slices.

5. Place under broiler until cheese is melted, about 2 minutes.

6. Serve with banana peppers, hot sauce or ketchup, if desired.

Honey-glazed Ginger Pork Meatballs

Servings: 6

Cooking Time: 20 Minutes

Ingredients:

- 1 ½ pounds ground pork
- 2 tablespoons finely chopped onion
- 3 cloves garlic, minced
- 1 teaspoon minced fresh ginger
- 1 teaspoon sesame oil
- 1 large egg
- 3 tablespoons panko bread crumbs
- Kosher salt and freshly ground black pepper
- HONEY GINGER SAUCE
- 2 tablespoons sesame oil
- 1 tablespoon canola or vegetable oil
- 3 cloves garlic, minced
- 1 ½ tablespoons minced fresh ginger
- 3 tablespoons unseasoned rice wine vinegar
- 1 tablespoon reduced-sodium soy sauce
- 3 tablespoons honey
- 2 to 3 teaspoons garlic chili sauce
- 1 teaspoon cornstarch
- 1 tablespoon cold water
- 2 tablespoons minced fresh cilantro

Directions:

1. Preheat the toaster oven to 375°F. Line a 12 x 12-inch baking pan with nonstick aluminum foil (or if lining the pan with regular foil, spray it with nonstick cooking spray).

2. Combine the pork, onion, garlic, ginger, sesame oil, egg, and panko bread crumbs in a large bowl. Season with salt and pepper. Form into meatballs about 1 ½ inches in diameter. Place the meatballs in the prepared baking pan. Bake for 18 to 20 minutes or until done and a meat thermometer registers 160°F.

3. Make the Honey Ginger Sauce: Combine the sesame oil, canola oil, garlic, and ginger in a medium skillet over medium-high heat. Cook, stirring frequently, for 1 minute. Add the vinegar, soy sauce, honey, and chili sauce and bring to a boil. Whisk the cornstarch with the water in a small bowl. Stir the cornstarch mixture into the sauce and cook, stirring constantly, until thickened. Add the meatballs to the skillet and coat with the sauce. Sprinkle with the cilantro for serving.

Miso-glazed Salmon With Broccoli

Servings: 2

Cooking Time: 25 Minutes

Ingredients:

- Nonstick cooking spray
- 2 tablespoons miso, preferably yellow
- 2 tablespoons mirin
- 1 tablespoon packed dark brown sugar
- 2 teaspoons minced fresh ginger
- 1 ½ teaspoons sesame oil
- 8 ounces fresh broccoli, cut into spears
- 1 tablespoon canola or vegetable oil
- Kosher salt and freshly ground black pepper
- 2 salmon fillets (5 to 6 ounces each)

Directions:

1. Preheat the toaster oven to 425°F. Spray a 12 x 12-inch baking pan with nonstick cooking spray.

2. Stir the miso, mirin, brown sugar, ginger, and sesame oil in a small bowl; set aside.

3. Toss the broccoli spears with the canola oil and season with salt and pepper. Place the broccoli on the pan. Bake, uncovered, for 10 minutes. Stir the broccoli and move to one side of the pan.

4. Place the salmon, skin side down, on the other end of the pan. Brush lightly with olive oil and season with salt and pepper. Bake for 10 minutes.

5. Brush the fish generously with the miso sauce. Bake for an additional 3 to 5 minutes, or until the fish flakes easily with a fork and a meat thermometer registers 145°F.

Favorite Baked Ziti

Servings: 4

Cooking Time: 30 Minutes

Ingredients:

- 2 tablespoons olive oil
- 1 small onion, diced
- 3 cloves garlic, minced
- ¼ teaspoon red pepper flakes
- 1 pound lean ground beef
- ½ teaspoon kosher salt
- ¼ cup dry red wine
- 1 (14.5-ounce) can crushed tomatoes
- 1 tablespoon tomato paste
- 16 ounces ziti, uncooked
- Nonstick cooking spray
- ⅓ cup grated Parmesan cheese
- 1 ½ cups shredded mozzarella cheese
- 2 ounces fresh mozzarella cheese, cut into cubes (about ½ cup)

Directions:

1. Heat the olive oil in a large skillet over medium-high heat. Add the onion and cook, stirring frequently, until tender, 3 to 4 minutes. Stir in the garlic and red pepper flakes. Add the ground beef and salt. Cook, breaking up the ground beef, until the meat is brown and cooked through. Drain well, if needed, and return to the skillet.

2. Add the wine and cook for 2 minutes. Add the tomatoes, tomato paste, and ¾ cup water.

Reduce the heat and simmer, uncovered, for 20 to 25 minutes, stirring occasionally.

3. Cook the ziti according to the package directions, except reduce the cooking time to 7 minutes. The ziti will be harder than Al Dente, which is what you want. Drain and rinse under cold water. Transfer to a large bowl.

4. Preheat the toaster oven to 425 ºF. Spray an 11 x 7 x 2 ½-inch baking dish with nonstick cooking spray. Spoon about 1 cup of the meat sauce into the prepared dish. Add half of the ziti in an even layer. Spoon about half of the remaining sauce over the ziti. Sprinkle with half the Parmesan and all the shredded mozzarella. Add the remaining half of ziti and cover with the remaining sauce. Sprinkle the remaining Parmesan on top.

5. Bake, covered, for 20 minutes. Remove from the oven and add the cubes of fresh mozzarella. Bake, uncovered, for an additional 10 minutes. If desired, turn to broil for a few minutes to make the top crispy and brown.

6. Remove from the oven and let stand for 10 minutes before serving.

Pork And Brown Rice Casserole

Servings: 4
Cooking Time: 45 Minutes

Ingredients:

- 2 very lean 6-ounce boneless pork chops, cut into 1-inch cubes
- ½ cup brown rice
- 1 cup chunky tomato sauce

- ½ cup dry white wine
- 3 tablespoons finely chopped onion
- 2 small zucchini squashes, finely chopped
- 2 plum tomatoes, chopped
- ½ teaspoon ground cumin
- ½ teaspoon ground ginger
- 1 teaspoon garlic powder
- 2 bay leaves
- Salt and freshly ground black pepper

Directions:

1. Preheat the toaster oven to 400° F.

2. Combine all the ingredients in a 1-quart 8½ × 8½ × 4-inch ovenproof baking dish. Cover with aluminum foil.

3. BAKE, covered, for 45 minutes, or until the rice is cooked to your preference. Discard the bay leaves before serving.

One-step Classic Goulash

Servings: 4
Cooking Time: 56 Minutes

Ingredients:

- 1 cup elbow macaroni
- 1 cup (8-ounce can) tomato sauce
- 1 cup very lean ground round or sirloin
- 1 cup peeled and chopped fresh tomato
- ½ cup finely chopped onion
- 1 teaspoon garlic powder
- Salt and freshly ground black pepper
- Topping:
- 1 cup homemade bread crumbs
- 1 tablespoon margarine

Directions:

1. Preheat the toaster oven to 400° F.

2. Combine all the ingredients, except the topping, with 2 cups water in a 1-quart 8½ × 8½ × 4-inch ovenproof baking dish and mix well. Adjust the seasonings to taste. Cover with aluminum foil.

3. BAKE, covered, for 50 minutes, or until the macaroni is cooked, stirring after 25 minutes to distribute the liquid. Uncover, sprinkle with bread crumbs, and dot with margarine.

4. BROIL for 6 minutes, or until the topping is lightly browned.

Scalloped Corn Casserole

Servings: 4
Cooking Time: 38 Minutes

Ingredients:
- Casserole mixture:
- 2 15-ounce cans corn
- 1 red bell pepper, chopped
- ¼ cup chopped scallions
- ½ cup fat-free half-and-half
- 2 tablespoons unbleached flour
- 2 eggs
- ½ teaspoon chili powder
- 1 teaspoon ground cumin
- 1 teaspoon garlic powder
- Salt and freshly ground black pepper to taste
- ¼ cup multigrain seasoned bread Crumbs
- 1 tablespoon margarine

Directions:
1. Preheat the toaster oven to 400° F.
2. Combine all the casserole mixture ingredients in a 1-quart 8½ × 8½ × 4-inch ovenproof baking

dish, mixing well. Adjust the seasonings to taste. Cover with aluminum foil.

3. BAKE, covered, for 30 minutes, or until the pepper and onions are tender. Remove from the oven and uncover. Sprinkle with the bread crumbs and dot with the margarine.

4. BROIL for 8 minutes, or until the bread crumb topping is lightly browned.

Salad Couscous

Servings: 4
Cooking Time: 10 Minutes

Ingredients:
- 1 10-ounce package precooked couscous
- 2 tablespoons olive oil
- Salt and freshly ground black pepper
- ¼ cup chopped fresh tomatoes
- 2 tablespoons chopped fresh basil leaves
- 1 tablespoon sliced almonds
- ½ bell pepper, chopped
- 3 scallions, chopped
- 2 tablespoons lemon juice

Directions:
1. Preheat the toaster oven to 400° F.
2. Mix together the couscous, 2 cups water, and olive oil in a 1-quart 8½ × 8½ × 4-inch ovenproof baking dish. Add salt and pepper to taste. Cover with aluminum foil.
3. BAKE, covered, for 10 minutes, or until the couscous is cooked. Remove from the oven, fluff with a fork and, when cool, add the tomatoes, basil leaves, almonds, pepper, scallions, and lemon juice. Adjust the seasonings to taste. Chill before serving.

Rosemary Lentils

Servings: 2

Cooking Time: 35 Minutes

Ingredients:

- ¼ cup lentils
- 1 tablespoon mashed Roasted Garlic
- 1 rosemary sprig
- 1 bay leaf
- Salt and freshly ground black pepper
- 2 tablespoons low-fat buttermilk
- 2 tablespoons tomato sauce

Directions:

1. Preheat the toaster oven to 400° F.

2. Combine the lentils, 1¼ cups water, garlic, rosemary sprig, and bay leaf in a 1-quart 8½ × 8½ × 4-inch ovenproof baking dish, stirring to blend well. Add the salt and pepper to taste. Cover with aluminum foil.

3. BAKE, covered, for 35 minutes, or until the lentils are tender. Remove the rosemary sprig and bay leaf and stir in the buttermilk and tomato sauce. Serve immediately.

Sheet Pan Loaded Nachos

Servings: 4

Cooking Time: 13 Minutes

Ingredients:

- 1 tablespoon canola or vegetable oil
- ½ pound lean ground beef
- ½ cup chopped onion
- 2 cloves garlic, minced
- 1 teaspoon chili powder
- ½ teaspoon ground cumin
- Kosher salt and freshly ground black pepper
- 6 ounces tortilla chips
- ½ cup canned black beans, rinsed and drained
- 1 ½ cups shredded sharp cheddar cheese or Mexican blend cheese
- ½ cup salsa
- Optional toppings: sliced jalapeño peppers, chopped bell peppers, sliced ripe olives, chopped tomatoes, minced fresh cilantro, sour cream, chopped avocado, guacamole, or chopped onion.

Directions:

1. Preheat the toaster oven to 400°F. Line a 12 x 12-inch baking pan with nonstick aluminum foil. (Or if lining the pan with regular foil, spray it with nonstick cooking spray.)

2. Heat the oil in a large skillet over medium-high heat. Add the ground beef and onion and cook, stirring frequently, until the beef is almost done. Add the garlic, chili powder, cumin, season with salt and pepper, and cook, stirring frequently, until the beef is fully cooked; drain.

3. Arrange the tortilla chips in an even layer in the prepared pan. Top with the beef-onion mixture, then top with the beans. Bake, uncovered, for 6 to 8 minutes. Top with the cheese and bake for 5 minutes more, or until the cheese is melted.

4. Drizzle with the salsa. Top as desired with any of the various toppings.

Family Favorite Pizza

Servings: 6

Cooking Time: 22 Minutes

Ingredients:

- CRUST
- ½ cup warm water (about 110 ºF)
- 1 teaspoon active dry yeast
- 1 ½ cups all-purpose flour, plus more for kneading
- 1 teaspoon kosher salt
- ½ teaspoon olive oil
- TOPPINGS
- Pizza sauce
- 2 cups shredded Italian blend cheese or mozzarella cheese
- ¼ cup grated Parmesan cheese
- Optional toppings: pepperoni slices, cooked crumbled or sliced sausage, vegetables, or other favorite pizza toppings

Directions:

1. Make the Crust: Pour the water into a medium bowl and sprinkle with the yeast. Let stand for 5 minutes until the yeast is foamy. Add the flour, salt, and olive oil. Mix until a dough forms. Turn the dough out on a floured surface and knead until a ball forms that springs back when you poke a finger into it, about 5 minutes. If the dough is too sticky, add a tablespoon of flour and knead into the dough. Cover the dough and allow to rest for 10 minutes.

2. Preheat the toaster oven to 450°F. Place a 12-inch pizza pan in the toaster oven while it is preheating.

3. Stretch and roll the dough into an 11 ½-inch round. If the dough starts to shrink back, let it rest for 5 to 10 more minutes and then continue to roll. Carefully remove the hot pan from the toaster oven and place the pizza crust on the hot pan. Top with the desired amount of sauce. Layer cheese and any of your favorite pizza toppings over the pizza.

4. Bake for 18 to 22 minutes, or until the crust is golden brown and the cheese is melted. Let stand for 5 minutes before cutting.

Kasha Loaf

Servings: 4

Cooking Time: 30 Minutes

Ingredients:

- 1 cup whole grain kasha
- 2 cups tomato sauce or 3 2 8-ounce cans tomato sauce (add a small amount of water to make 4 2 cups)
- 3 tablespoons minced onion or scallions
- 1 tablespoon minced garlic
- 1 cup multigrain bread crumbs
- 1 egg
- 1 teaspoon paprika
- 1 teaspoon chili powder
- 1 teaspoon sesame oil

Directions:

1. Preheat the toaster oven to 400° F.

2. Combine all the ingredients in a bowl and transfer to an oiled or nonstick regular-size 4½ × 8½ × 2/4-inch loaf pan.

3. BAKE, uncovered, for 30 minutes, or until lightly browned.

Easy Oven Lasagne

Servings: 4

Cooking Time: 60 Minutes

Ingredients:

- 6 uncooked lasagna noodles, broken in half
- 1 15-ounce jar marinara sauce
- ½ pound ground turkey or chicken breast
- ½ cup part-skim ricotta cheese
- ½ cup shredded part-skim mozzarella cheese
- 2 tablespoons chopped fresh oregano leaves or 1 teaspoon dried oregano
- 2 tablespoons chopped fresh basil leaves or 1 teaspoon dried basil
- 1 tablespoon garlic cloves, minced
- ¼ cup grated Parmesan cheese
- Salt and freshly ground black pepper to taste

Directions:

1. Preheat the toaster oven to 375° F.

2. Layer in a 1-quart 8½ × 8½ × 4-inch ovenproof baking dish in this order: 6 lasagna noodle halves, ½ jar of the marinara sauce, ½ cup water, half of the ground meat, half of the ricotta and mozzarella cheeses, half of the oregano and basil leaves, and half of the minced garlic. Repeat the layer, starting with the noodles. Cover the dish with aluminum foil.

3. BAKE, covered, for 50 minutes, or until the noodles are tender. Uncover, sprinkle the top with Parmesan cheese and bake for another 10 minutes, or until the liquid is reduced and the top is browned.

Baked Parsleyed Cheese Grits

Servings: 4

Cooking Time: 30 Minutes

Ingredients:

- 4 strips lean uncooked turkey bacon, cut in half
- 1 cup grits
- 2 cups skim or low-fat soy milk
- 1 egg
- ½ cup shredded Parmesan cheese
- 1 tablespoon chopped fresh parsley
- ½ teaspoon garlic powder
- Salt and butcher's pepper to taste

Directions:

1. Preheat the toaster oven to 350° F.

2. Layer an 8½ × 8½ × 2-inch square baking (cake) pan with the bacon strips.

3. Combine the remaining ingredients in a medium bowl and pour the mixture over the strips.

4. BAKE, uncovered, for 30 minutes, or until the grits are cooked. Cut into squares with a spatula and serve.

Herbal Summer Casserole

Servings: 4

Cooking Time: 45 Minutes

Ingredients:

- 4 small yellow (summer) squashes, cut into ¾-inch slices
- 1 green bell pepper, seeded and chopped

- 1 tablespoon roasted garlic, mashed in 1 tablespoon olive oil
- ¼ cup seasoned bread crumbs
- ¼ cup grated Parmesan cheese
- ¼ cup chopped fresh parsley
- 2 tablespoons chopped fresh cilantro
- 2 tablespoons chopped onion
- 2 plum tomatoes, chopped
- 2 carrots, peeled and cut into ¼-inch slices
- 4 tablespoons fresh lemon juice
- ½ teaspoon caraway seeds
- ¼ teaspoon celery seed
- Salt and freshly ground black pepper to taste

Directions:

1. Preheat the toaster oven to 400° F.

2. Combine all the ingredients in a 1-quart 8½ × 8½ × 4-inch ovenproof baking dish, mixing well. Cover the dish with aluminum foil.

3. BAKE, covered, for 45 minutes, or until the vegetables are tender.

Oven-baked Barley

Servings: 2

Cooking Time: 60 Minutes

Ingredients:

- ⅓ cup barley, toasted
- Seasonings:
- 1 tablespoon sesame oil
- 1 tablespoon sesame seeds
- ¼ teaspoon ground cumin
- ¼ teaspoon turmeric
- ½ teaspoon garlic powder
- Salt and freshly ground black pepper to taste

Directions:

1. Combine the barley and 1½ cups water in a 1-quart 8½ × 8½ × 4-inch ovenproof baking dish. Cover with aluminum foil.

2. BAKE, covered, for 50 minutes, or until almost cooked, testing the grains after 30 minutes for softness.

3. Add the oil and seasonings and fluff with a fork to combine. Cover and let the barley sit for 10 minutes to finish cooking and absorb the flavors of the seasonings. Fluff once more before serving.

SNACKS APPETIZERS AND SIDES

Beet Chips

Servings: 4

Cooking Time: 20 Minutes

Ingredients:

- 2 large red beets, washed and skinned
- 1 tablespoon avocado oil
- ¼ teaspoon salt

Directions:

1. Preheat the toaster oven to 330°F.

2. Using a mandolin or sharp knife, slice the beets in ⅛-inch slices. Place them in a bowl of water and let them soak for 30 minutes. Drain the water and pat the beets dry with a paper towel or kitchen cloth.

3. In a medium bowl, toss the beets with avocado oil and sprinkle them with salt.

4. Lightly spray the air fryer oven with olive oil mist and place the beet chips into the air fryer oven. To allow for even cooking, don't overlap the beets; cook in batches if necessary.

5. Cook the beet chips 15 to 20 minutes, rotate every 5 minutes, until the outer edges of the beets begin to flip up like a chip. Remove from the air fryer oven and serve warm. Repeat with the remaining chips until they're all cooked.

Elote

Servings: 2

Cooking Time: 45 Minutes

Ingredients:

- 2 ears corn, husks and silk removed, stalks left intact
- 1 teaspoon extra-virgn olive oil
- 3 tablespoons mayonnaise
- 1 tablespoon crumbled queso fresco
- 1 tablespoon minced fresh cilantro
- 1 teaspoon lime juice, plus lime wedges for serving
- 1 small garlic clove, minced
- ¼ teaspoon chili powder
- Pinch table salt

Directions:

1. Adjust toaster oven rack to middle position, select broiler function, and heat broiler. Brush corn all over with oil and transfer to small aluminum foil–lined rimmed baking sheet. Broil corn until well browned on 1 side, 15 to 20 minutes. Flip corn and broil until browned on opposite side, 15 to 20 minutes.

2. Meanwhile, whisk mayonnaise, queso fresco, cilantro, lime juice, garlic, chili powder, and salt in bowl until incorporated. Remove corn from oven and brush evenly on all sides with mayonnaise mixture. Season with salt and pepper to taste. Serve corn with lime wedges and any extra mayonnaise mixture.

Cheese Straws

Servings: 8

Cooking Time: 7 Minutes

Ingredients:

- For dusting All-purpose flour
- Two quarters of one thawed sheet (that is, a half of the sheet cut into two even pieces; wrap and refreeze the remainder) A 17.25-ounce box frozen puff pastry
- 1 Large egg(s)
- 2 tablespoons Water
- ¼ cup (about ¾ ounce) Finely grated Parmesan cheese
- up to 1 teaspoon Ground black pepper

Directions:

1. Preheat the toaster oven to 400°F.

2. Dust a clean, dry work surface with flour. Set one of the pieces of puff pastry on top, dust the pastry lightly with flour, and roll with a rolling pin to a 6-inch square.

3. Whisk the egg(s) and water in a small or medium bowl until uniform. Brush the pastry square(s) generously with this mixture. Sprinkle each square with 2 tablespoons grated cheese and up to ½ teaspoon ground black pepper.

4. Cut each square into 4 even strips. Grasp each end of 1 strip with clean, dry hands; twist it into a cheese straw. Place the twisted straws on a baking sheet.

5. Lay as many straws as will fit in the air-fryer oven—as a general rule, 4 of them in a small machine, 5 in a medium model, or 6 in a large. There should be space for air to circulate around the straws. Set the baking sheet with any remaining straws in the fridge.

6. Air-fry undisturbed for 7 minutes, or until puffed and crisp. Use tongs to transfer the cheese straws to a wire rack, then make subsequent batches in the same way (keeping the baking sheet with the remaining straws in the fridge as each batch cooks). Serve warm.

Arancini With Sun-dried Tomatoes And Mozzarella

Servings: 6

Cooking Time: 15 Minutes

Ingredients:

- 1 tablespoon olive oil
- ½ small onion, finely chopped
- 1 cup Arborio rice
- ¼ cup white wine or dry vermouth
- 1 cup vegetable or chicken stock
- 1½ cups water
- 1 teaspoon salt
- freshly ground black pepper
- ⅓ cup grated Parmigiano-Reggiano cheese
- 2 to 3 ounces mozzarella cheese
- 2 eggs, lightly beaten
- ¼ cup chopped oil-packed sun-dried tomatoes
- 1½ cups Italian seasoned breadcrumbs, divided
- olive oil
- marinara sauce, for serving

Directions:

1. .Start by cooking the Arborio rice.

2. Stovetop Method: Preheat a medium saucepan over medium heat. Add the olive oil and sauté the onion until it starts to become tender – about 5 minutes. Add the rice and stir well to coat all the grains of rice. Add the white wine or vermouth. Let this simmer and get absorbed by the rice. Then add the stock and water, cover, reduce the heat to low and simmer for 20 minutes.

3. Pressure-Cooker Method: Preheat the pressure cooker using the BROWN setting. Add the oil and cook the onion for a few minutes. Add the rice, wine, stock, water, salt and freshly ground black pepper, give everything one good stir and lock the lid in place. Pressure cook on HIGH for 7 minutes. Reduce the pressure with the QUICK-RELEASE method and carefully remove the lid.

4. Taste the rice to make sure it is tender. Season with salt and freshly ground black pepper and stir in the grated Parmigiano-Reggiano cheese. Spread the rice out onto a baking sheet to cool.

5. While the rice is cooling, cut the mozzarella into ¾-inch cubes.

6. Once the rice has cooled, combine the rice with the eggs, sun-dried tomatoes and ½ cup of the breadcrumbs. Place the remaining breadcrumbs in a shallow dish. Shape the rice mixture into 12 balls. Press a hole in the rice ball with your finger and push one or two cubes of mozzarella cheese into the hole. Mold the rice back into a ball, enclosing the cheese. Roll the finished rice balls in the breadcrumbs and place them on a baking sheet while you make the remaining rice balls. Spray or brush the rice balls with olive oil.

7. Preheat the toaster oven to 380°F.

8. Cook 6 arancini at a time. Air-fry for 10 minutes. Gently turn the arancini over, brush or spray with oil again and air-fry for another 5 minutes. Serve warm with the marinara sauce.

Broiled Maryland Crabcakes With Creamy Herb Sauce

Servings: 8-9

Cooking Time: 8 Minutes

Ingredients:

- 1 large egg
- 3 Tablespoons mayonnaise
- 1 Tablespoon brown mustard
- 1 Tablespoon all-purpose flour
- 1 teaspoon seafood seasoning
- 1/2 teasoon salt
- 1/4 teaspoon ground black pepper
- 1 pound lump crabmeat
- 1/4 cup chopped parsley
- 1 small shallot, minced
- 1 garlic clove, minced
- Creamy Herb Sauce

Directions:

1. In a medium bowl, mix egg, mayonnaise, mustard, flour, seafood seasoning, salt and pepper until well blended.

2. Stir in crabmeat, parsley, shallots and garlic until crab is coated with mayonnaise mixture.

3. Place 1/4 cup crab mixture on broiler pan; lightly press down. Repeat with remaining mixture.

4. Set toaster oven on BROIL. Broil crabcakes 8 minutes, without turning.

5. Serve with Creamy Herb Sauce.

Warm And Salty Edamame

Servings: 4

Cooking Time: 10 Minutes

Ingredients:

- 1 pound Unshelled edamame
- Vegetable oil spray
- ¾ teaspoon Coarse sea salt or kosher salt

Directions:

1. Preheat the toaster oven to 400°F.

2. Place the edamame in a large bowl and lightly coat them with vegetable oil spray. Toss well, spray again, and toss until they are evenly coated.

3. When the machine is at temperature, pour the edamame into the air fryer oven and air-fry, tossing the pan quite often to rearrange the edamame, for 7 minutes, or until warm and aromatic. (Air-fry for 10 minutes if the edamame were frozen and not thawed.)

4. Pour the edamame into a bowl and sprinkle the salt on top. Toss well, then set aside for a couple of minutes before serving with an empty bowl on the side for the pods.

Baked Brie And Cranberry Bites

Servings: 24

Cooking Time: 10 Minutes

Ingredients:

- 4 ounces triple creme brie
- 1/4 cup Cranberry Orange Relish
- 4 sheets phyllo pastry sheets, thawed
- 1/4 cup butter, melted

Directions:

1. Preheat the toaster oven to 400°F.

2. Cut brie into 1/4-inch slices, then in 1-inch pieces; set aside.

3. Unroll and cover the phyllo sheets with plastic wrap and then a slightly damp towel to prevent drying out. On a large cutting board, place one sheet of phyllo. Lightly brush with melted butter. Continue to layer phyllo sheets and brush with butter, but do not butter the top of the last sheet.

4. Cut the layered phyllo sheets into 24 equal squares. Place each square in a mini-muffin pan, pushing down center to form a cup. Keep cut squares and already shaped phyllo cups covered with plastic wrap and a damp towel to prevent drying out while shaping more squares.

5. Place a piece of brie in each phyllo cup in muffin pans. Top with 1/2 teaspoon cranberry relish.

6. Bake 8 to 10 minutes or until golden brown.

Spinach And Artichoke Dip

Servings: 6

Cooking Time: 45 Minutes

Ingredients:

- 6 ounces cream cheese, softened
- ½ cup mayonnaise
- 2 tablespoons water

- 1 tablespoon lemon juice
- 3 garlic cloves, minced
- ¼ teaspoon table salt
- ¼ teaspoon pepper
- 3 cups jarred whole baby artichokes packed in water, rinsed, patted dry, and chopped
- 10 ounces frozen spinach, thawed and squeezed dry
- 2 tablespoons minced fresh chives

Directions:

1. Adjust toaster oven rack to middle position and preheat the toaster oven to 400 degrees. Whisk cream cheese, mayonnaise, water, lemon juice, garlic, salt, and pepper in large bowl until well combined. Gently fold in artichokes and spinach. Transfer mixture to 2-quart baking dish and smooth top with rubber spatula.

2. Bake until spotty golden brown and bubbling around edges, 20 to 25 minutes. Transfer dish to wire rack and let cool for 10 minutes. Sprinkle with chives and serve.

Breaded Zucchini

Servings: 4
Cooking Time: 10 Minutes

Ingredients:

- 1 cup all-purpose flour
- 2 large eggs
- 1½ cups panko bread crumbs
- ½ cup grated Parmesan cheese
- Sea salt, for seasoning
- Freshly ground black pepper, for seasoning
- Oil spray (hand-pumped)

- 2 zucchini, cut into ¼-inch slices

Directions:

1. Preheat the toaster oven on AIR FRY to 350°F for 5 minutes.

2. Sprinkle the flour onto a plate.

3. In a small bowl, beat the eggs and place the bowl next to the flour.

4. In a medium bowl, stir the bread crumbs and cheese and season the mixture with salt and pepper. Place the bowl next to the eggs.

5. Place the air-fryer basket on the baking sheet and generously spray the rack with oil.

6. Dredge a zucchini slice in the flour, then the eggs, then the bread crumb mixture until well coated. Place the slice in the basket and repeat with the remaining zucchini slices. Spray the slices on both sides with oil.

7. In position 2, air fry for 10 minutes, turning once at 5 minutes, until golden brown and crispy. Serve immediately.

Polenta Fries With Chili-lime Mayo

Servings: 4
Cooking Time: 28 Minutes

Ingredients:

- 2 teaspoons vegetable or olive oil
- ¼ teaspoon paprika
- 1 pound prepared polenta, cut into 3-inch x ½-inch sticks
- salt and freshly ground black pepper
- Chili-Lime Mayo
- ½ cup mayonnaise

- 1 teaspoon chili powder
- ¼ teaspoon ground cumin
- juice of half a lime
- 1 teaspoon chopped fresh cilantro
- salt and freshly ground black pepper

Directions:

1. Preheat the toaster oven to 400°F.

2. Combine the oil and paprika and then carefully toss the polenta sticks in the mixture.

3. Air-fry the polenta fries at 400°F for 15 minutes. Rotate the fries and continue to air-fry for another 13 minutes or until the fries have browned nicely. Season to taste with salt and freshly ground black pepper.

4. To make the chili-lime mayo, combine all the ingredients in a small bowl and stir well.

5. Serve the polenta fries warm with chili-lime mayo on the side for dipping.

Eggs In Avocado Halves

Servings: 3

Cooking Time: 23 Minutes

Ingredients:

- 3 Hass avocados, halved and pitted but not peeled
- 6 Medium eggs
- Vegetable oil spray
- 3 tablespoons Heavy or light cream (not fat-free cream)
- To taste Table salt
- To taste Ground black pepper

Directions:

1. Preheat the toaster oven to 350°F .

2. Slice a small amount off the (skin) side of each avocado half so it can sit stable, without rocking. Lightly coat the skin of the avocado half (the side that will now sit stable) with vegetable oil spray.

3. Arrange the avocado halves open side up on a cutting board, then crack an egg into the indentation in each where the pit had been. If any white overflows the avocado half, wipe that bit of white off the cut edge of the avocado before proceeding.

4. Remove the pan (or its attachment) from the machine and set the filled avocado halves in it in one layer. Return it to the machine without pushing it in. Drizzle each avocado half with about 1½ teaspoons cream, a little salt, and a little ground black pepper.

5. Air-fry undisturbed for 10 minutes for a soft-set yolk, or air-fry for 13 minutes for more-set eggs.

6. Use a nonstick-safe spatula and a flatware fork for balance to transfer the avocado halves to serving plates. Cool a minute or two before serving.

Beef Satay With Peanut Dipping Sauce

Servings: 4

Cooking Time: 60 Minutes

Ingredients:

- SKEWERS
- 1 pound flank steak, trimmed
- 2 tablespoons soy sauce

- 2 tablespoons vegetable oil
- 2 tablespoons packed dark brown sugar
- 2 tablespoons minced fresh cilantro
- 2 scallions, sliced thin
- 1½ tablespoons ketchup
- 1 garlic clove, minced
- ½ teaspoon sriracha
- SPICY PEANUT DIPPING SAUCE
- ¼ cup peanut butter (creamy or chunky)
- 2 tablespoons hot water, plus extra as needed
- 1½ tablespoons lime juice
- 1 scallion, sliced thin
- 1 tablespoon ketchup
- 1½ teaspoons soy sauce
- 1½ teaspoons packed dark brown sugar
- 1½ teaspoons minced fresh cilantro
- ¾ teaspoon sriracha
- 1 garlic clove, minced

Directions:

1. FOR THE SKEWERS: Slice beef against grain ¼ inch thick (you should have at least 20 slices).

2. Combine soy sauce, oil, sugar, cilantro, scallions, ketchup, garlic, and sriracha in medium bowl; add beef; and toss to combine. Cover and refrigerate for 15 minutes. Weave 1 beef slice evenly onto each skewer, leaving at least 1 inch at bottom of skewer exposed (Skewers can be refrigerated for up to 24 hours.)

3. FOR THE SPICY PEANUT DIPPING SAUCE: Whisk peanut butter and hot water together in medium bowl. Stir in lime juice, scallion, ketchup, soy sauce, sugar, cilantro, sriracha, and garlic. Adjust consistency with extra hot water as needed; set aside for serving.

4. Adjust toaster oven rack to middle position, select broiler function, and heat broiler. Set small wire rack in aluminum foil–lined small rimmed baking sheet and spray rack with vegetable oil spray. Arrange skewers in two rows across width of prepared rack with all exposed skewer ends facing center of rack. Cover skewer ends in center of sheet with strip of foil and secure by crimping tightly at edges. Broil skewers until beef is no longer pink on top, 2 to 3 minutes. Flip skewers and continue to broil until beef is fully cooked and spotty brown, 4 to 6 minutes. Serve with peanut sauce.

Sweet Plantain Chips

Servings: 4

Cooking Time: 11 Minutes

Ingredients:

- 2 Very ripe plantain(s), peeled and sliced into 1-inch pieces
- Vegetable oil spray
- 3 tablespoons Maple syrup
- For garnishing Coarse sea salt or kosher salt

Directions:

1. Pour about ½ cup water into the bottom of your air fryer oven or into a metal tray on a lower rack in some models. Preheat the toaster oven to 400°F.

2. Put the plantain pieces in a bowl, coat them with vegetable oil spray, and toss gently, spraying

at least one more time and tossing repeatedly, until the pieces are well coated.

3. When the machine is at temperature, arrange the plantain pieces in the air fryer oven in one layer. Air-fry undisturbed for 5 minutes.

4. Remove the pan from the machine and spray the back of a metal spatula with vegetable oil spray. Use the spatula to press down on the plantain pieces, spraying it again as needed, to flatten the pieces to about half their original height. Brush the plantain pieces with maple syrup, then return the pan to the machine and continue air-frying undisturbed for 6 minutes, or until the plantain pieces are soft and caramelized.

5. Use kitchen tongs to transfer the pieces to a serving platter. Sprinkle the pieces with salt and cool for a couple of minutes before serving. Or cool to room temperature before serving, about 1 hour.

Caramelized Onion Dip

Servings: 2

Cooking Time: 20 Minutes

Ingredients:

- 1 tablespoon unsalted butter
- 1 tablespoon olive oil
- 1 large sweet onion, quartered and very thinly sliced crosswise
- Kosher salt
- 1 clove garlic, minced
- 3 tablespoons dry white wine
- ½ teaspoon dried thyme leaves
- ½ teaspoon freshly ground black pepper
- 1 baguette, thinly sliced
- Nonstick cooking spray
- 1 cup shredded Gruyère or Swiss cheese
- ½ cup sour cream
- ½ cup mayonnaise
- ¼ cup shredded Parmesan cheese
- 3 strips bacon, cooked until crisp and crumbled

Directions:

1. Melt the butter and olive oil in a large skillet over medium heat. Add the onion and season with salt. Cook, stirring frequently, for 3 minutes. Reduce the heat to low and cook, stirring occasionally, for 20 to 25 minutes, or until the onions are a deep golden brown color.

2. Increase the heat to medium. Stir in the garlic, wine, thyme, and pepper. Cook, stirring frequently, for 3 minutes or until the wine has mostly evaporated. Remove from the heat.

3. Meanwhile, toast the baguette slices in the toaster oven until golden brown and crisp; set aside.

4. Preheat the toaster oven to 350°F. Spray a 1-quart casserole with nonstick cooking spray.

5. Stir the Gruyère, sour cream, mayonnaise, Parmesan, and bacon into the onions. Spoon the mixture into the prepared casserole dish. Cover and bake for 20 minutes or until hot and the cheese is melted. Allow to stand for 5 to 10 minutes before serving. To serve, spoon the warm onion-cheese mixture onto the toast.

Crispy Tofu Bites

Servings: 4

Cooking Time: 20 Minutes

Ingredients:

- 1 pound Extra firm unflavored tofu
- Vegetable oil spray

Directions:

1. Wrap the piece of tofu in a triple layer of paper towels. Place it on a wooden cutting board and set a large pot on top of it to press out excess moisture. Set aside for 10 minutes.

2. Preheat the toaster oven to 400°F.

3. Remove the pot and unwrap the tofu. Cut it into 1-inch cubes. Place these in a bowl and coat them generously with vegetable oil spray. Toss gently, then spray generously again before tossing, until all are glistening.

4. Gently pour the tofu pieces into the air fryer oven, spread them into as close to one layer as possible, and air-fry for 20 minutes, using kitchen tongs to gently rearrange the pieces at the 7- and 14-minute marks, until light brown and crisp.

5. Gently pour the tofu pieces onto a wire rack. Cool for 5 minutes before serving warm.

Chicken Shawarma Bites

Servings: 6

Cooking Time: 22 Minutes

Ingredients:

- 1½ pounds Boneless skinless chicken thighs, trimmed of any fat and cut into 1-inch pieces
- 1½ tablespoons Olive oil
- Up to 1½ tablespoons Minced garlic
- ½ teaspoon Table salt
- ¼ teaspoon Ground cardamom
- ¼ teaspoon Ground cinnamon
- ¼ teaspoon Ground cumin
- ¼ teaspoon Mild paprika
- Up to a ¼ teaspoon Grated nutmeg
- ¼ teaspoon Ground black pepper

Directions:

1. Preheat the toaster oven to 400°F.

2. Mix all the ingredients in a large bowl until the chicken is thoroughly and evenly coated in the oil and spices.

3. When the machine is at temperature, scrape the coated chicken pieces into the air fryer oven and spread them out into one layer as much as you can. Air-fry for 22 minutes, rotate at least three times during cooking to rearrange the pieces, until well browned and crisp.

4. Pour the chicken pieces onto a wire rack. Cool for 5 minutes before serving.

Savory Sausage Balls

Servings: 10

Cooking Time: 8 Minutes

Ingredients:

- 2 cups all-purpose flour
- 1 tablespoon baking powder
- ½ teaspoon garlic powder
- ¼ teaspoon onion powder
- ½ teaspoon salt
- 3 tablespoons milk
- 2½ cups grated pepper jack cheese

- 1 pound fresh sausage, casing removed

Directions:

1. Preheat the toaster oven to 370°F.

2. In a large bowl, whisk together the flour, baking powder, garlic powder, onion powder, and salt. Add in the milk, grated cheese, and sausage.

3. Using a tablespoon, scoop out the sausage and roll it between your hands to form a rounded ball. You should end up with approximately 32 balls. Place them in the air fryer oven in a single layer and working in batches as necessary.

4. Air-fry for 8 minutes, or until the outer coating turns light brown.

5. Carefully remove, repeating with the remaining sausage balls.

Sugar-glazed Walnuts

Servings: 6

Cooking Time: 5 Minutes

Ingredients:

- 1 Large egg white(s)
- 2 tablespoons Granulated white sugar
- ⅛ teaspoon Table salt
- 2 cups (7 ounces) Walnut halves

Directions:

1. Preheat the toaster oven to 400°F.

2. Use a whisk to beat the egg white(s) in a large bowl until quite foamy, more so than just well combined but certainly not yet a meringue.

3. If you're working with the quantities for a small batch, remove half of the foamy egg white.

4. If you're working with the quantities for a large batch, remove a quarter of it. It's fine to eyeball the amounts.

5. You can store the removed egg white in a sealed container to save for another use.

6. Stir in the sugar and salt. Add the walnut halves and toss to coat evenly and well, including the nuts' crevasses.

7. When the machine is at temperature, use a slotted spoon to transfer the walnut halves to the air fryer oven, taking care not to dislodge any coating. Gently spread the nuts into as close to one layer as you can. Air-fry undisturbed for 2 minutes.

8. Break up any clumps, toss the walnuts gently but well, and air-fry for 3 minutes more, tossing after 1 minute, then every 30 seconds thereafter, until the nuts are browned in spots and very aromatic. Watch carefully so they don't burn.

9. Gently dump the nuts onto a lipped baking sheet and spread them into one layer. Cool for at least 10 minutes before serving, separating any that stick together. The walnuts can be stored in a sealed container at room temperature for up to 5 days.

Fried Green Tomatoes

Servings: 4

Cooking Time: 15 Minutes

Ingredients:

- 2 eggs
- ¼ cup buttermilk
- ½ cup cornmeal

- ½ cup breadcrumbs
- ¼ teaspoon salt
- 1½ pounds firm green tomatoes, cut in ¼-inch slices
- oil for misting or cooking spray
- Horseradish Drizzle
- ¼ cup mayonnaise
- ¼ cup sour cream
- 2 teaspoons prepared horseradish
- ½ teaspoon Worcestershire sauce
- ½ teaspoon lemon juice
- ⅛ teaspoon black pepper

Directions:

1. Mix all ingredients for Horseradish Drizzle together and chill while you prepare the green tomatoes.

2. Preheat the toaster oven to 390°F.

3. Beat the eggs and buttermilk together in a shallow bowl.

4. Mix cornmeal, breadcrumbs, and salt together in a plate or shallow dish.

5. Dip 4 tomato slices in the egg mixture, then roll in the breadcrumb mixture.

6. Mist one side with oil and place in air fryer oven, oil-side down, in a single layer.

7. Mist the top with oil.

8. Air-fry for 15 minutes, turning once, until brown and crispy.

9. Repeat steps 5 through 8 to cook remaining tomatoes.

10. Drizzle horseradish sauce over tomatoes just before serving.

Sausage Cheese Pinwheels

Servings: 16

Cooking Time: 22 Minutes

Ingredients:

- 1 sheet frozen puff pastry, about 9 inches square, thawed (½ of a 17.3-ounce package)
- ½ pound bulk sausage
- ¾ cup shredded cheddar cheese

Directions:

1. Preheat the toaster oven to 400°F. Grease a 12 x 12-inch baking pan.

2. Unfold the puff pastry on a lightly floured surface and roll into a 10 x 12-inch rectangle. Carefully spread the sausage over the surface of the rectangle to within ½ inch of all four edges. Sprinkle the cheese evenly over the sausage. Starting with the long side, roll up tightly and press the edges to seal.

3. Using a serrated knife, slice the roll into ½-inch-thick pieces. You will get about 16 slices. Place the slices, cut side up, in the prepared baking pan. Bake for 18 to 22 minutes or until golden and the sausage is cooked through.

4. Serve warm or at room temperature.

Fried Mozzarella Sticks

Servings: 7

Cooking Time: 5 Minutes

Ingredients:

- 7 1-ounce string cheese sticks, unwrapped
- ½ cup All-purpose flour or tapioca flour
- 2 Large egg(s), well beaten

- 2¼ cups Seasoned Italian-style dried bread crumbs (gluten-free, if a concern)
- Olive oil spray

Directions:

1. Unwrap the string cheese and place the pieces in the freezer for 20 minutes (but not longer, or they will be too frozen to soften in the time given in the air fryer oven).

2. Preheat the toaster oven to 400°F.

3. Set up and fill three shallow soup plates or small pie plates on your counter: one for the flour, one for the egg(s), and one for the bread crumbs.

4. Dip a piece of cold string cheese in the flour until well coated (keep the others in the freezer). Gently tap off any excess flour, then set the stick in the egg(s). Roll it around to coat, let any excess egg mixture slip back into the rest, and set the stick in the bread crumbs. Gently roll it around to coat it evenly, even the ends. Now dip it back in the egg(s), then again in the bread crumbs, rolling it to coat well and evenly. Set the stick aside on a cutting board and coat the remaining pieces of string cheese in the same way.

5. Lightly coat the sticks all over with olive oil spray. Place them in the air fryer oven in one layer and air-fry undisturbed for 5 minutes, or until golden brown and crisp.

6. Remove from the machine and cool for 5 minutes. Use a nonstick-safe spatula to transfer the mozzarella sticks to a serving platter. Serve hot.

Cinnamon Pita Chips

Servings: 4

Cooking Time: 6 Minutes

Ingredients:

- 2 tablespoons sugar
- 2 teaspoons cinnamon
- 2 whole 6-inch pitas, whole grain or white
- oil for misting or cooking spray

Directions:

1. Mix sugar and cinnamon together.

2. Cut each pita in half and each half into 4 wedges. Break apart each wedge at the fold.

3. Mist one side of pita wedges with oil or cooking spray. Sprinkle them all with half of the cinnamon sugar.

4. Turn the wedges over, mist the other side with oil or cooking spray, and sprinkle with the remaining cinnamon sugar.

5. Place pita wedges in air fryer oven and air-fry at 330°F for 2 minutes.

6. Cook 2 more minutes. If needed cook 2 more minutes, until crisp. Watch carefully because at this point they will cook very quickly.

Parmesan Crisps

Servings: 6

Cooking Time: 7 Minutes

Ingredients:

- 6 tablespoons shredded Parmesan cheese

Directions:

1. Preheat the toaster oven to 350°F on BAKE for 10 minutes.

2. Line the baking tray with a silicone mat or parchment paper.

3. Place the Parmesan by tablespoons about 2 inches apart on the tray, spreading the cheese out in an even layer about 2½ inches in diameter.

4. Place the try in position 2 and bake for 7 minutes until the edges are browned, and the cheese is no longer bubbling.

5. Remove from the oven and allow to cool on the rack for 10 minutes before serving.

Korean "fried" Chicken Wings

Servings: 4
Cooking Time: 25 Minutes

Ingredients:

- Wings Ingredients
- 2 pounds chicken wings
- 1 teaspoon kosher salt
- ½ teaspoon black pepper
- 1½ teaspoons onion powder
- 1½ teaspoons garlic powder
- ¾ teaspoons ground mustard
- 1 teaspoon gochugaru
- 2 tablespoons cornstarch
- 1 tablespoon water
- Cooking spray
- Toasted sesame seeds, for sprinkling
- Sauce Ingredients
- 3 tablespoons Korean gojuchang red pepper paste
- 2 tablespoon white distilled vinegar
- 1 tablespoon hot water
- 2 tablespoons honey
- 1 tablespoon soy sauce

Directions:

1. Combine all the ingredients for the wings except the cooking spray and sesame seeds in a large bowl. Mix well.

2. Preheat the toaster oven to 400°F.

3. Spray both sides of the wings with cooking spray.

4. Place the wings into the fry basket, then insert the basket at mid position in the preheated oven.

5. Select the Air Fry function, adjust time to 25 minutes, then press Start/Pause.

6. Mix together sauce ingredients until well combined, then microwave on high for 30 seconds. Set aside.

7. Remove wings when done, then place the wings and sauce in a large bowl and toss together until the wings are well coated.

8. Sprinkle the wings with toasted sesame seeds and serve.

Golden Fried Cauliflower

Servings: 4
Cooking Time: 40 Minutes

Ingredients:

- 1 small head cauliflower, cut into small florets
- 1 tablespoon olive oil
- Sea salt, for seasoning
- Freshly ground black pepper, for seasoning
- 2 teaspoons fresh parsley, chopped, for garnish

Directions:

1. Preheat the toaster oven to 375°F on AIR FRY for 5 minutes.

2. In a large bowl, toss the cauliflower and olive oil until the florets are well coated. Season with salt and pepper.

3. Place the air-fryer basket in the baking tray. Spread half the florets in the basket and air fry in position 2 for 20 minutes, shaking the basket after 10 minutes, until the cauliflower is golden and crispy. Transfer the cauliflower to a serving bowl and repeat with the remaining cauliflower. Cover the first batch loosely with foil to keep it warm while you cook the second batch.

4. Top with the parsley and serve.

POULTRY

Peanut Butter-barbeque Chicken

Servings: 4

Cooking Time: 20 Minutes

Ingredients:

- 1 pound boneless, skinless chicken thighs
- salt and pepper
- 1 large orange
- ½ cup barbeque sauce
- 2 tablespoons smooth peanut butter
- 2 tablespoons chopped peanuts for garnish (optional)
- cooking spray

Directions:

1. Season chicken with salt and pepper to taste. Place in a shallow dish or plastic bag.

2. Grate orange peel, squeeze orange and reserve 1 tablespoon of juice for the sauce.

3. Pour remaining juice over chicken and marinate for 30 minutes.

4. Mix together the reserved 1 tablespoon of orange juice, barbeque sauce, peanut butter, and 1 teaspoon grated orange peel.

5. Place ¼ cup of sauce mixture in a small bowl for basting. Set remaining sauce aside to serve with cooked chicken.

6. Preheat the toaster oven to 360°F. Spray air fryer oven with nonstick cooking spray.

7. Remove chicken from marinade, letting excess drip off. Place in air fryer oven and air-fry for 5 minutes. Turn chicken over and cook 5 minutes longer.

8. Brush both sides of chicken lightly with sauce.

9. Cook chicken 5 minutes, then turn thighs one more time, again brushing both sides lightly with sauce. Air-fry for 5 more minutes or until chicken is done and juices run clear.

10. Serve chicken with remaining sauce on the side and garnish with chopped peanuts if you like.

East Indian Chicken

Servings: 4

Cooking Time: 45 Minutes

Ingredients:

- Sauce mixture:
- ¼ cup white wine
- ¼ cup red wine
- ½ cup low-sodium vegetable broth
- ½ cup finely chopped onion
- ½ cup finely chopped bell pepper
- ½ cup finely chopped fresh tomato
- 3 garlic cloves, minced
- 1 tablespoon peeled and minced fresh ginger
- 2 teaspoons curry powder
- ¼ teaspoon ground cinnamon
- ¼ teaspoon ground cumin
- 4 small dried chilies
- Salt and freshly ground black pepper to taste
- 6 skinless, boneless chicken thighs

Directions:

1. Preheat the toaster oven to 400° F.

2. Combine the sauce mixture ingredients in a 1-quart 8½ × 8½ × 4-inch ovenproof baking dish and mix well. Add the chicken and toss together to coat well. Cover the dish with aluminum foil.

3. BAKE for 45 minutes, or until the chicken is tender. Uncover and spoon the sauce over the chicken. Remove the chilies before serving.

Crispy Duck With Cherry Sauce

Servings: 2

Cooking Time: 33 Minutes

Ingredients:

- 1 whole duck (up to 5 pounds), split in half, back and rib bones removed
- 1 teaspoon olive oil
- salt and freshly ground black pepper
- Cherry Sauce:
- 1 tablespoon butter
- 1 shallot, minced
- ½ cup sherry
- ¾ cup cherry preserves 1 cup chicken stock
- 1 teaspoon white wine vinegar
- 1 teaspoon fresh thyme leaves
- salt and freshly ground black pepper

Directions:

1. Preheat the toaster oven to 400°F.

2. Trim some of the fat from the duck. Rub olive oil on the duck and season with salt and pepper. Place the duck halves in the air fryer oven, breast side up and facing the center of the air fryer oven.

3. Air-fry the duck for 20 minutes. Turn the duck over and air-fry for another 6 minutes.

4. While duck is air-frying, make the cherry sauce. Melt the butter in a large sauté pan. Add the shallot and sauté until it is just starting to brown – about 2 to 3 minutes. Add the sherry and deglaze the pan by scraping up any brown bits from the bottom of the pan. Simmer the liquid for a few minutes, until it has reduced by half. Add the cherry preserves, chicken stock and white wine vinegar. Whisk well to combine all the ingredients. Simmer the sauce until it thickens and coats the back of a spoon – about 5 to 7 minutes. Season with salt and pepper and stir in the fresh thyme leaves.

5. When the air fryer oven timer goes off, spoon some cherry sauce over the duck and continue to air-fry at 400°F for 4 more minutes. Then, turn the duck halves back over so that the breast side is facing up. Spoon more cherry sauce over the top of the duck, covering the skin completely. Air-fry for 3 more minutes and then remove the duck to a plate to rest for a few minutes.

6. Serve the duck in halves, or cut each piece in half again for a smaller serving. Spoon any additional sauce over the duck or serve it on the side.

Gluten-free Nutty Chicken Fingers

Servings: 4

Cooking Time: 10 Minutes

Ingredients:

- ½ cup gluten-free flour
- ½ teaspoon garlic powder

- ¼ teaspoon onion powder
- ¼ teaspoon black pepper
- ¼ teaspoon salt
- 1 cup walnuts, pulsed into coarse flour
- ½ cup gluten-free breadcrumbs
- 2 large eggs
- 1 pound boneless, skinless chicken tenders

Directions:

1. Preheat the toaster oven to 400°F.

2. In a medium bowl, mix the flour, garlic, onion, pepper, and salt. Set aside.

3. In a separate bowl, mix the walnut flour and breadcrumbs.

4. In a third bowl, whisk the eggs.

5. Liberally spray the air fryer oven with olive oil spray.

6. Pat the chicken tenders dry with a paper towel. Dredge the tenders one at a time in the flour, then dip them in the egg, and toss them in the breadcrumb coating. Repeat until all tenders are coated.

7. Set each tender in the air fryer oven, leaving room on each side of the tender to allow for flipping.

8. When the air fryer oven is full, cook 5 minutes, flip, and cook another 5 minutes. Check the internal temperature after cooking completes; it should read 165°F. If it does not, cook another 2 to 4 minutes.

9. Remove the tenders and let cool 5 minutes before serving. Repeat until all the tenders are cooked.

Chicken Chunks

Servings: 4

Cooking Time: 10 Minutes

Ingredients:

- 1 pound chicken tenders cut in large chunks, about 1½ inches
- salt and pepper
- ½ cup cornstarch
- 2 eggs, beaten
- 1 cup panko breadcrumbs
- oil for misting or cooking spray

Directions:

1. Season chicken chunks to your liking with salt and pepper.

2. Dip chicken chunks in cornstarch. Then dip in egg and shake off excess. Then roll in panko crumbs to coat well.

3. Spray all sides of chicken chunks with oil or cooking spray.

4. Place chicken in air fryer oven in single layer and air-fry at 390°F for 5 minutes. Spray with oil, turn chunks over, and spray other side.

5. Air-fry for an additional 5 minutes or until chicken juices run clear and outside is golden brown.

6. Repeat steps 4 and 5 to cook remaining chicken.

Fiesta Chicken Plate

Servings: 4

Cooking Time: 15 Minutes

Ingredients:

- 1 pound boneless, skinless chicken breasts (2 large breasts)
- 2 tablespoons lime juice
- 1 teaspoon cumin
- ½ teaspoon salt
- ½ cup grated Pepper Jack cheese
- 1 16-ounce can refried beans
- ½ cup salsa
- 2 cups shredded lettuce
- 1 medium tomato, chopped
- 2 avocados, peeled and sliced
- 1 small onion, sliced into thin rings
- sour cream
- tortilla chips (optional)

Directions:

1. Split each chicken breast in half lengthwise.

2. Mix lime juice, cumin, and salt together and brush on all surfaces of chicken breasts.

3. Place in air fryer oven and air-fry at 390°F for 15 minutes, until well done.

4. Divide the cheese evenly over chicken breasts and air-fry for an additional minute to melt cheese.

5. While chicken is cooking, heat refried beans on stovetop or in microwave.

6. When ready to serve, divide beans among 4 plates. Place chicken breasts on top of beans and spoon salsa over. Arrange the lettuce, tomatoes, and avocados artfully on each plate and scatter with the onion rings.

7. Pass sour cream at the table and serve with tortilla chips if desired.

Chicken Pot Pie

Servings: 4

Cooking Time: 65 Minutes

Ingredients:

- ¼ cup salted butter
- 1 small sweet onion, chopped
- 1 carrot, chopped
- 1 teaspoon minced garlic
- ¼ cup all-purpose flour
- 1 cup low-sodium chicken broth
- ¼ cup heavy (whipping) cream
- 2 cups diced store-bought rotisserie chicken
- 1 cup frozen peas
- Sea salt, for seasoning
- Freshly ground black pepper, for seasoning
- 1 unbaked store-bought pie crust

Directions:

1. Place the rack in position 1 and preheat the toaster oven to 350°F on BAKE for 5 minutes.

2. Melt the butter in a large saucepan over medium-high heat. Sauté the onion, carrot, and garlic until softened, about 12 minutes. Whisk in the flour to form a thick paste and whisk for 1 minute to cook.

3. Add the broth and whisk until thickened, about 2 minutes. Add the heavy cream, whisking to combine. Add the chicken and peas, and season with salt and pepper.

4. Transfer the filling to a 1½-quart casserole dish and top with the pie crust, tucking the edges into the sides of the casserole dish to completely enclose the filling. Cut 4 or 5 slits in the top of the crust.

5. Bake for 50 minutes until the crust is golden brown and the filling is bubbly. Serve.

Foiled Rosemary Chicken Breasts

Servings: 2

Cooking Time: 30 Minutes

Ingredients:

- 2 skinless, boneless chicken breast halves
- Sauce:
- 3 tablespoons dry white wine
- 1 tablespoon Dijon mustard
- 2 tablespoons nonfat plain yogurt
- Salt and freshly ground black pepper to taste
- 2 rosemary sprigs

Directions:

1. Preheat the toaster oven to 400° F.

2. Place each breast on a 12 × 12-inch square of heavy-duty aluminum foil (or regular foil doubled) and turn up the edges of the foil.

3. Mix together the sauce ingredients and spoon over the chicken breasts. Lay a rosemary sprig on each breast. Bring up the edges of the foil and fold to form a sealed packet.

4. BAKE for 25 minutes or until juices run clear when the meat is pierced with a fork. Remove the rosemary sprigs.

5. BROIL for 5 minutes, or until lightly browned. Replace the sprigs and serve.

Chicken Wellington

Servings: 4

Cooking Time: 30 Minutes

Ingredients:

- 2 small (5- to 6-ounce) boneless, skinless chicken breast halves
- Kosher salt and freshly ground black pepper
- 2 teaspoons Italian seasoning
- 2 tablespoons olive oil
- 3 tablespoons unsalted butter, softened
- 3 ounces cream cheese, softened (about ⅓ cup)
- ¾ cup shredded Monterey Jack cheese
- ¼ cup grated Parmesan cheese
- 1 cup frozen (loose-pack) chopped spinach, thawed and squeezed dry
- ¾ cup chopped canned artichoke hearts, drained
- ½ teaspoon garlic powder
- 1 sheet frozen puff pastry, about 9 inches square, thawed (½ of a 17.3-ounce package)
- 1 large egg, lightly beaten

Directions:

1. Preheat the toaster oven to 425° F. Line a 12 x 12-inch baking pan with parchment paper.

2. Cut the chicken breasts in half lengthwise. Season each piece with the salt, pepper, and Italian seasoning. Fold the thinner end under the larger piece to make the chicken breasts into a rounded shape. Secure with toothpicks.

3. Heat a large skillet over medium-high heat. Add the olive oil and heat. Add the chicken breasts and brown well, turning to brown evenly.

Remove from the skillet and set aside to cool. Remove the toothpicks.

4. Stir the butter, cream cheese, Monterey Jack, and Parmesan in a large bowl. Stir in the spinach, artichoke hearts, and garlic powder. Season with salt and pepper.

5. Roll out the puff pastry sheet on a lightly floured board until it makes a 12-inch square. Cut into four equal pieces. Spread one-fourth of the spinach-artichoke mixture on the surface of each pastry square to within ½ inch of all four edges. Place the chicken in the center of each. Gently fold the puff pastry up over the chicken and pinch the edges to seal tightly.

6. Place each chicken bundle, seam side down, on the prepared pan. Brush the top of each bundle lightly with the beaten egg. Bake for 25 to 30 minutes, or until the pastry is golden brown and crisp and a meat thermometer inserted into the chicken reaches 165°F.

Fried Chicken

Servings: 4

Cooking Time: 40 Minutes

Ingredients:

- 12 skin-on chicken drumsticks
- 1 cup buttermilk
- 1½ cups all-purpose flour
- 1 tablespoon smoked paprika
- ¾ teaspoon celery salt
- ¾ teaspoon dried mustard
- ½ teaspoon garlic powder
- ½ teaspoon freshly ground black pepper
- ½ teaspoon sea salt
- ½ teaspoon dried thyme
- ¼ teaspoon dried oregano
- 4 large eggs
- Oil spray (hand-pumped)

Directions:

1. Place the chicken and buttermilk in a medium bowl, cover, and refrigerate for at least 1 hour, up to overnight.

2. Preheat the toaster oven to 375°F on AIR FRY for 5 minutes.

3. In a large bowl, stir the flour, paprika, celery salt, mustard, garlic powder, pepper, salt, thyme, and oregano until well mixed.

4. Beat the eggs until frothy in a medium bowl and set them beside the flour.

5. Place the air-fryer basket in the baking tray and generously spray it with the oil.

6. Dredge a chicken drumstick in the flour, then the eggs, and then in the flour again, thickly coating it, and place the drumstick in the basket. Repeat with 5 more drumsticks and spray them all lightly with the oil on all sides.

7. In position 2, air fry for 20 minutes, turning halfway through, until golden brown and crispy with an internal temperature of 165°F.

8. Repeat with the remaining chicken, covering the cooked chicken loosely with foil to keep it warm. Serve.

Tender Chicken Meatballs

Servings: 4

Cooking Time: 30 Minutes

Ingredients:

- 1 pound lean ground chicken
- ½ cup bread crumbs
- 1 large egg
- 1 scallion, both white and green parts, finely chopped
- ¼ cup whole milk
- ¼ cup shredded, unsweetened coconut
- 1 tablespoon low-sodium soy sauce
- 1 teaspoon minced garlic
- 1 teaspoon fresh ginger, peeled and grated
- Pinch cayenne powder
- Oil spray (hand-pumped)

Directions:

1. Preheat the toaster oven to 375°F on BAKE for 5 minutes.

2. Line the baking tray with parchment and set aside.

3. In a large bowl, mix the chicken, bread crumbs, egg, scallion, milk, coconut, soy sauce, garlic, ginger, and cayenne until very well combined.

4. Shape the chicken mixture into 1½-inch balls and place them in a single layer on the baking tray. Do not overcrowd them.

5. In position 2, bake for 20 minutes, turning halfway through, until they are cooked through and evenly browned. Serve.

Tasty Meat Loaf

Servings: 4

Cooking Time: 35 Minutes

Ingredients:

- 1 to 1½ pounds ground turkey or chicken breast
- 1 egg
- 1 tablespoon chopped fresh parsley
- 2 tablespoons chopped bell pepper
- 3 tablespoons chopped canned mushrooms
- 2 tablespoons chopped onion
- 2 garlic cloves, minced
- ½ cup multigrain bread crumbs
- 1 tablespoon Worcestershire sauce
- 1 tablespoon ketchup
- Freshly ground black pepper to taste

Directions:

1. Preheat the toaster oven to 400° F.

2. Combine all the ingredients in a large bowl and press into a regular-size 4½ × 8½ × 2¼-inch loaf pan.

3. BAKE for 35 minutes, or until browned on top.

Tandoori Chicken Legs

Servings: 2

Cooking Time: 30 Minutes

Ingredients:

- 1 cup plain yogurt
- 2 cloves garlic, minced
- 1 tablespoon grated fresh ginger
- 2 teaspoons paprika

- 2 teaspoons ground coriander
- 1 teaspoon ground turmeric
- 1 teaspoon salt
- ¼ teaspoon ground cayenne pepper
- juice of 1 lime
- 2 bone-in, skin-on chicken legs
- fresh cilantro leaves

Directions:

1. Make the marinade by combining the yogurt, garlic, ginger, spices and lime juice. Make slashes into the chicken legs to help the marinade penetrate the meat. Pour the marinade over the chicken legs, cover and let the chicken marinate for at least an hour or overnight in the refrigerator.

2. Preheat the toaster oven oven to 380°F.

3. Transfer the chicken legs from the marinade to the air fryer oven, reserving any extra marinade. Air-fry for 15 minutes. Flip the chicken over and pour the remaining marinade over the top. Air-fry for another 15 minutes, watching to make sure it doesn't brown too much. If it does start to get too brown, you can loosely tent the chicken with aluminum foil, tucking the ends of the foil under the chicken to stop it from blowing around.

4. Serve over rice with some fresh cilantro on top.

Roast Chicken

Servings: 6

Cooking Time: 90 Minutes

Ingredients:

- Nonstick cooking spray
- 1 whole (3 ½ -pound) chicken

- Grated zest and juice of 1 lemon
- 1 tablespoon olive oil
- 1 ½ teaspoons kosher salt
- 1 teaspoon garlic powder
- ½ teaspoon dried thyme leaves
- ½ teaspoon freshly ground black pepper

Directions:

1. Preheat the toaster oven to 350°F. Spray a 12 x 12-inch baking pan with nonstick cooking spray.

2. Drizzle the chicken cavity with about half of the lemon juice. Place half of the juiced lemon into the chicken cavity. Truss the chicken using kitchen twine.

3. Rub the chicken evenly with the olive oil.

4. Stir the salt, garlic powder, lemon zest, thyme, and pepper in a small bowl. Using your fingertips, rub the seasonings evenly over the chicken. Place the chicken, breast side up, in the prepared pan. Drizzle with the remaining lemon juice.

5. Roast, uncovered, for 1 ¼ hours to 1 ½ hours, or until a meat thermometer registers 165°F. Let stand for 10 minutes before carving.

Curry Powder

Servings: 1

Cooking Time: 5 Minutes

Ingredients:

- ½ cup coriander seeds
- 2 tablespoons ground cumin
- 2 tablespoons black peppercorns
- 1 tablespoon sesame seeds
- 1 tablespoon cardamom seeds, extracted from the pods

- 2 small dried chili peppers
- 3 tablespoons turmeric
- 2 tablespoons ground ginger

Directions:

1. Combine the coriander seeds, cumin, peppercorns, sesame seeds, cardamom seeds, and chili peppers in an oiled or nonstick 8½ × 8½ × 2-inch square baking (cake) pan.

2. TOAST once, then turn with tongs and toast again, or continue toasting and turning until evenly toasted. Cool and grind the spices in a blender until the mixture becomes a powder. Add the turmeric and ground ginger and mix well. Store in a covered container in the refrigerator.

Italian Roasted Chicken Thighs

Servings: 6
Cooking Time: 14 Minutes

Ingredients:

- 6 boneless chicken thighs
- ½ teaspoon dried oregano
- ½ teaspoon garlic powder
- ½ teaspoon sea salt
- ½ teaspoon black pepper
- ¼ teaspoon crushed red pepper flakes

Directions:

1. Pat the chicken thighs with paper towel.

2. In a small bowl, mix the oregano, garlic powder, salt, pepper, and crushed red pepper flakes. Rub the spice mixture onto the chicken thighs.

3. Preheat the toaster oven to 400°F.

4. Place the chicken thighs in the air fryer oven and spray with cooking spray. Air-fry for 10 minutes, turn over, and cook another 4 minutes. When cooking completes, the internal temperature should read 165°F.

Jerk Chicken Drumsticks

Servings: 2
Cooking Time: 20 Minutes

Ingredients:

- 1 or 2 cloves garlic
- 1 inch of fresh ginger
- 2 serrano peppers, (with seeds if you like it spicy, seeds removed for less heat)
- 1 teaspoon ground allspice
- 1 teaspoon ground nutmeg
- 1 teaspoon chili powder
- ½ teaspoon dried thyme
- ½ teaspoon ground cinnamon
- ½ teaspoon paprika
- 1 tablespoon brown sugar
- 1 teaspoon soy sauce
- 2 tablespoons vegetable oil
- 6 skinless chicken drumsticks

Directions:

1. Combine all the ingredients except the chicken in a small chopper or blender and blend to a paste. Make slashes into the meat of the chicken drumsticks and rub the spice blend all over the chicken (a pair of plastic gloves makes this really easy). Transfer the rubbed chicken to a non-reactive covered container and let the

chicken marinate for at least 30 minutes or overnight in the refrigerator.

2. Preheat the toaster oven to 400°F.

3. Transfer the drumsticks to the air fryer oven. Air-fry for 10 minutes. Turn the drumsticks over and air-fry for another 10 minutes. Serve warm with some rice and vegetables or a green salad.

Crispy "fried" Chicken

Servings: 4
Cooking Time: 14 Minutes

Ingredients:

- ¾ cup all-purpose flour
- ½ teaspoon paprika
- ¼ teaspoon black pepper
- ¼ teaspoon salt
- 2 large eggs
- 1½ cups panko breadcrumbs
- 1 pound boneless, skinless chicken tenders

Directions:

1. Preheat the toaster oven to 400°F.

2. In a shallow bowl, mix the flour with the paprika, pepper, and salt.

3. In a separate bowl, whisk the eggs; set aside.

4. In a third bowl, place the breadcrumbs.

5. Liberally spray the air fryer oven with olive oil spray.

6. Pat the chicken tenders dry with a paper towel. Dredge the tenders one at a time in the flour, then dip them in the egg, and toss them in the breadcrumb coating. Repeat until all tenders are coated.

7. Set each tender in the air fryer oven, leaving room on each side of the tender to allow for flipping.

8. When the air fryer oven is full, cook 4 to 7 minutes, flip, and cook another 4 to 7 minutes.

9. Remove the tenders and let cool 5 minutes before serving. Repeat until all tenders are cooked.

Coconut Chicken With Apricot-ginger Sauce

Servings: 4
Cooking Time: 8 Minutes

Ingredients:

- 1½ pounds boneless, skinless chicken tenders, cut in large chunks (about 1¼ inches)
- salt and pepper
- ½ cup cornstarch
- 2 eggs
- 1 tablespoon milk
- 3 cups shredded coconut (see below)
- oil for misting or cooking spray
- Apricot-Ginger Sauce
- ½ cup apricot preserves
- 2 tablespoons white vinegar
- ¼ teaspoon ground ginger
- ¼ teaspoon low-sodium soy sauce
- 2 teaspoons white or yellow onion, grated or finely minced

Directions:

1. Mix all ingredients for the Apricot-Ginger Sauce well and let sit for flavors to blend while you cook the chicken.

2. Season chicken chunks with salt and pepper to taste.

3. Place cornstarch in a shallow dish.

4. In another shallow dish, beat together eggs and milk.

5. Place coconut in a third shallow dish. (If also using panko breadcrumbs, as suggested below, stir them to mix well.)

6. Spray air fryer oven with oil or cooking spray.

7. Dip each chicken chunk into cornstarch, shake off excess, and dip in egg mixture.

8. Shake off excess egg mixture and roll lightly in coconut or coconut mixture. Spray with oil.

9. Place coated chicken chunks in air fryer oven in a single layer, close together but without sides touching.

10. Air-fry at 360°F for 4 minutes, stop, and turn chunks over.

11. Cook an additional 4 minutes or until chicken is done inside and coating is crispy brown.

12. Repeat steps 9 through 11 to cook remaining chicken chunks.

Hot Thighs

Servings: 4

Cooking Time: 40 Minutes

Ingredients:

- 6 skinless, boneless chicken thighs
- ¼ cup fresh lemon juice
- Seasonings:
- 1 teaspoon garlic powder
- ¼ teaspoon cayenne
- ½ teaspoon chili powder
- 1 teaspoon onion powder
- Salt and freshly ground black pepper to taste

Directions:

1. Preheat the toaster oven to 450° F.

2. Brush the chicken thighs liberally with the lemon juice. Set aside.

3. Combine the seasonings in a small bowl and transfer to a paper or plastic bag. Add the thighs and shake well to coat. Remove from the bag and place in an oiled or nonstick 8½ × 8½ × 2-inch square (cake) pan. Cover the pan with aluminum foil.

4. BAKE, covered, for 20 minutes. Turn the pieces with tongs and bake again for another 20 minutes, or until the meat is tender and lightly browned.

Buffalo Egg Rolls

Servings: 8

Cooking Time: 9 Minutes

Ingredients:

- 1 teaspoon water
- 1 tablespoon cornstarch
- 1 egg
- 2½ cups cooked chicken, diced or shredded (see opposite page)
- ⅓ cup chopped green onion
- ⅓ cup diced celery
- ⅓ cup buffalo wing sauce
- 8 egg roll wraps
- oil for misting or cooking spray
- Blue Cheese Dip
- 3 ounces cream cheese, softened

- ⅓ cup blue cheese, crumbled
- 1 teaspoon Worcestershire sauce
- ¼ teaspoon garlic powder
- ¼ cup buttermilk (or sour cream)

Directions:

1. Mix water and cornstarch in a small bowl until dissolved. Add egg, beat well, and set aside.

2. In a medium size bowl, mix together chicken, green onion, celery, and buffalo wing sauce.

3. Divide chicken mixture evenly among 8 egg roll wraps, spooning ½ inch from one edge.

4. Moisten all edges of each wrap with beaten egg wash.

5. Fold the short ends over filling, then roll up tightly and press to seal edges.

6. Brush outside of wraps with egg wash, then spritz with oil or cooking spray.

7. Place 4 egg rolls in air fryer oven.

8. Air-fry at 390°F for 9 minutes or until outside is brown and crispy.

9. While the rolls are cooking, prepare the Blue Cheese Dip. With a fork, mash together cream cheese and blue cheese.

10. Stir in remaining ingredients.

11. Dip should be just thick enough to slightly cling to egg rolls. If too thick, stir in buttermilk or milk 1 tablespoon at a time until you reach the desired consistency.

12. Cook remaining 4 egg rolls as in steps 7 and 8.

13. Serve while hot with Blue Cheese Dip, more buffalo wing sauce, or both.

Marinated Green Pepper And Pineapple Chicken

Servings: 4

Cooking Time: 20 Minutes

Ingredients:

- Marinade:
- 1 teaspoon finely chopped fresh ginger
- 2 garlic cloves, finely chopped
- 1 teaspoon toasted sesame oil
- 1 tablespoon brown sugar
- 2 tablespoons soy sauce
- ¾ cup dry white wine
- 2 skinless, boneless chicken breasts, cut into 1 × 3-inch strips
- 2 tablespoons chopped onion
- 1 bell pepper, chopped
- 1 5-ounce can pineapple chunks, drained
- 2 tablespoons grated unsweetened coconut

Directions:

1. Combine the marinade ingredients in a medium bowl and blend well. Add the chicken strips and spoon the mixture over them. Marinate in the refrigerator for at least 1 hour. Remove the strips from the marinade and place in an oiled or nonstick 8½ × 8½ × 2-inch square (cake) pan. Add the onion and pepper and mix well.

2. BROIL for 8 minutes. Then remove from the oven and, using tongs, turn the chicken, pepper, and onion pieces. (Spoon the reserved marinade over the pieces, if desired.)

3. BROIL again for 8 minutes, or until the chicken, pepper, and onion are cooked through

and tender. Add the pineapple chunks and coconut and toss to mix well.

4. BROIL for another 4 minutes, or until the coconut is lightly browned.

Orange-glazed Roast Chicken

Servings: 6
Cooking Time: 100 Minutes

Ingredients:
- 1 3-pound whole chicken, rinsed and patted dry with paper towels
- Brushing mixture:
- 2 tablespoons orange juice concentrate
- 1 tablespoon soy sauce
- 1 tablespoon toasted sesame oil
- 1 teaspoon ground ginger
- Salt and freshly ground black pepper to taste

Directions:
1. Preheat the toaster oven to 400° F.
2. Place the chicken, breast side up, in an oiled or nonstick 8½ × 8½ × 2-inch square (cake) pan and brush with the mixture, which has been combined in a small bowl, reserving the remaining mixture. Cover with aluminum foil.
3. BAKE for 1 hour and 20 minutes. Uncover and brush the chicken with remaining mixture.
4. BAKE, uncovered, for 20 minutes, or until the breast is tender when pierced with a fork and golden brown.

Roasted Game Hens With Vegetable Stuffing

Servings: 2

Cooking Time: 50 Minutes

Ingredients:
- Stuffing:
- 1 cup multigrain bread crumbs
- 2 tablespoons chopped onion
- 1 carrot, shredded
- 1 celery stalk, shredded
- 1 garlic clove, minced
- 2 tablespoons chopped fresh parsley
- Salt and freshly ground black pepper to taste
- 2 whole game hens (thawed or fresh), giblets removed, rinsed, and patted dry with paper towels

Directions:
1. Preheat the toaster oven to 350° F.
2. Combine the stuffing ingredients in a medium bowl. Stuff the cavities of the game hens and place them in a baking dish.
3. BAKE, covered, for 45 minutes, or until the meat is tender and the juices run clear when the breast is pierced with a fork.
4. BROIL, uncovered, for 8 minutes, or until lightly browned.

Chicken Potpie

Servings: 4
Cooking Time: 48 Minutes

Ingredients:
- Pie filling:
- 1 tablespoon unbleached flour
- ½ cup evaporated skim milk
- 4 skinless, boneless chicken thighs, cut into 1-inch cubes

- 1 cup potatoes, peeled and cut into ½-inch pieces
- ½ cup frozen green peas
- ½ cup thinly sliced carrot
- 2 tablespoons chopped onion
- ½ cup chopped celery
- 1 teaspoon garlic powder
- Salt and freshly ground black pepper to taste
- 8 sheets phyllo pastry, thawed Olive oil

Directions:

1. Preheat the toaster oven to 400° F.

2. Whisk the flour into the milk until smooth in a 1-quart 8½ × 8½ × 4-inch ovenproof baking dish. Add the remaining filling ingredients and mix well. Adjust the seasonings to taste. Cover the dish with aluminum foil.

3. BAKE for 40 minutes, or until the carrot, potatoes, and celery are tender. Remove from the oven and uncover.

4. Place one sheet of phyllo pastry on top of the baked pie-filling mixture, bending the edges to fit the shape of the baking dish. Brush the sheet with olive oil. Add another sheet on top of it and brush with oil. Continue adding the remaining sheets, brushing each one, until the crust is completed. Brush the top with oil.

5. BAKE for 6 minutes, or until the phyllo pastry is browned.

DESSERTS

Mississippi Mud Brownies

Servings: 16
Cooking Time: 34 Minutes

Ingredients:

- Nonstick cooking spray
- 3 tablespoons unsweetened cocoa powder
- ¼ cup canola or vegetable oil
- ¼ cup unsalted butter, softened
- 1 cup granulated sugar
- 2 large eggs
- 1 teaspoon pure vanilla extract
- ¾ cup all-purpose flour
- ½ teaspoon table salt
- ½ cup pecan pieces, toasted
- 2 cups mini marshmallows
- FROSTING
- ¼ cup unsalted butter, melted
- 3 tablespoons unsweetened cocoa powder
- ½ teaspoon pure vanilla extract
- 2 cups confectioners' sugar
- 2 to 3 tablespoons whole milk

Directions:

1. Preheat the toaster oven to 350°F. Spray an 8-inch square baking pan with nonstick cooking spray.

2. Beat the cocoa and oil in a large bowl with a handheld mixer at medium speed. Add the butter and mix until smooth. Beat in the granulated sugar. Add the eggs, one at a time, mixing after each addition. Add the vanilla and mix. On low speed, blend in the flour and salt. Stir in the pecans.

3. Pour the batter into the prepared pan. Bake for 28 to 32 minutes, or until a wooden pick inserted into the center comes out clean.

4. Remove the brownies from the oven and sprinkle the marshmallows over the top. Return to the oven and bake for about 2 minutes or until the marshmallows are puffed. Place on a wire rack and let cool completely.

5. Meanwhile, make the frosting: Combine the butter, cocoa, vanilla, confectioners' sugar, and 2 tablespoons milk in a large bowl. Beat until smooth. If needed for the desired consistency, add additional milk. Frost the cooled brownies.

Cheese Blintzes

Servings: 6
Cooking Time: 10 Minutes

Ingredients:

- 1½ 7½-ounce package(s) farmer cheese
- 3 tablespoons Regular or low-fat cream cheese (not fat-free)
- 3 tablespoons Granulated white sugar
- ¼ teaspoon Vanilla extract
- 6 Egg roll wrappers
- 3 tablespoons Butter, melted and cooled

Directions:

1. Preheat the toaster oven to 375°F.

2. Use a flatware fork to mash the farmer cheese, cream cheese, sugar, and vanilla in a small bowl until smooth.

3. Set one egg roll wrapper on a clean, dry work surface. Place ¼ cup of the filling at the edge closest to you, leaving a ½-inch gap before the edge of the wrapper. Dip your clean finger in water and wet the edges of the wrapper. Fold the perpendicular sides over the filling, then roll the wrapper closed with the filling inside. Set it aside seam side down and continue filling the remainder of the wrappers.

4. Brush the wrappers on all sides with the melted butter. Be generous. Set them seam side down in the air fryer oven with as much space between them as possible. Air-fry undisturbed for 10 minutes, or until lightly browned.

5. Use a nonstick-safe spatula to transfer the blintzes to a wire rack. Cool for at least 5 minutes or up to 20 minutes before serving.

Cowboy Cookies

Servings: 3
Cooking Time: 14 Minutes

Ingredients:

- Recommended Hamilton Beach® Product: Stand Mixers
- 1 cup butter
- 1 cup sugar
- 1 cup light brown sugar
- 2 eggs
- 2 cups flour
- 1 teaspoon baking soda
- ½ teaspoon baking powder
- ½ teaspoon salt
- 2 cups oatmeal
- 1 tablespoon vanilla
- 12 ounces chocolate chips
- 1 ½ cups coconut

Directions:

1. Preheat the toaster oven to 350°F.

2. With flat beater attachment, cream together butter, sugar, and brown sugar at a medium setting until well blended. Mix in vanilla and eggs. Reduce speed and gradually add flour, baking soda, baking powder, and salt mix until smooth.

3. On a low setting, mix in oatmeal, chocolate chips, and coconut until well mixed. Drop rounded spoon full onto ungreased cookie sheet.

4. Bake on middle rack of oven for 12 to 14 minutes.

Almond-roasted Pears

Servings: 4
Cooking Time: 15 Minutes

Ingredients:

- Yogurt Topping
- 1 container vanilla Greek yogurt (5–6 ounces)
- ¼ teaspoon almond flavoring
- 2 whole pears
- ¼ cup crushed Biscoff cookies (approx. 4 cookies)
- 1 tablespoon sliced almonds
- 1 tablespoon butter

Directions:

1. Stir almond flavoring into yogurt and set aside while preparing pears.

2. Halve each pear and spoon out the core.

3. Place pear halves in air fryer oven.

4. Stir together the cookie crumbs and almonds. Place a quarter of this mixture into the hollow of each pear half.

5. Cut butter into 4 pieces and place one piece on top of crumb mixture in each pear.

6. Preheat the toaster oven to 400°F and air-fry for 15 minutes or until pears have cooked through but are still slightly firm.

7. Serve pears warm with a dollop of yogurt topping.

Green Grape Meringues

Servings: 4

Cooking Time: 40 Minutes

Ingredients:

- 1 cup sugar
- 3 egg whites, beaten until stiff
- ½ teaspoon lemon juice
- Vanilla frozen yogurt
- 1 cup sliced fresh green grapes
- 2 squares unsweetened baking chocolate, shaved
- Nonfat whipped topping

Directions:

1. Preheat the toaster oven to 250° F.

2. Add the sugar slowly to the egg white mixture and continue to beat. Add the lemon juice. With a tablespoon, drop on an oiled or nonstick 6½ × 10-inch baking sheet to make a mound of meringue approximately 2 inches across. Make a slight depression in the center of each one.

3. BAKE for 40 minutes, or until crusty and browned. Cool and fill each meringue shell with a scoop of vanilla frozen yogurt. Top with equal portions of green grapes, chocolate shavings, and nonfat whipped topping. The meringues may be stored in an airtight container until ready to use.

Lime Cheesecake

Servings: 6

Cooking Time: 30 Minutes

Ingredients:

- Oil spray (hand-pumped)
- ½ cup graham cracker crumbs
- 24 ounces cream cheese, room temperature
- 1½ cups granulated sugar
- 4 large eggs
- ¼ cup sour cream
- Juice and zest of 1 lime
- 2 teaspoons vanilla extract

Directions:

1. Place the rack in position 1 and preheat the oven to 350°F on BAKE for 5 minutes.

2. Lightly spray an 8-inch springform pan with the oil and spread the graham cracker crumbs in the bottom.

3. Bake for 10 minutes, then remove the crust from the air fryer and set it aside.

4. In a large bowl, beat the cream cheese until very smooth with an electric hand beater. Add the sugar by ½-cup measures, beating very well after

each addition and scraping down the sides of the bowl.

5.   Add the eggs one at a time, beating well after each addition and scraping down the sides of the bowl.

6.   Beat in the sour cream, lime juice, lime zest, and vanilla until very well blended and fluffy, about 4 minutes.

7.   Transfer the batter to the pan and smooth the top.

8.   Bake for 30 minutes or until set.

9.   Let the cheesecake cool in the oven for 30 minutes and then transfer to the refrigerator to cool completely. Serve.

Giant Oatmeal–peanut Butter Cookie

Servings: 4

Cooking Time: 18 Minutes

Ingredients:

* 1 cup Rolled oats (not quick-cooking or steel-cut oats)
* ½ cup All-purpose flour
* ½ teaspoon Ground cinnamon
* ½ teaspoon Baking soda
* ⅓ cup Packed light brown sugar
* ¼ cup Solid vegetable shortening
* 2 tablespoons Natural-style creamy peanut butter
* 3 tablespoons Granulated white sugar
* 2 tablespoons (or 1 small egg, well beaten) Pasteurized egg substitute, such as Egg Beaters
* ⅓ cup Roasted, salted peanuts, chopped
* Baking spray

Directions:

1.   Preheat the toaster oven to 350°F..

2.   Stir the oats, flour, cinnamon, and baking soda in a bowl until well combined.

3.   Using an electric hand mixer at medium speed, beat the brown sugar, shortening, peanut butter, granulated white sugar, and egg substitute or egg (as applicable) until smooth and creamy, about 3 minutes, scraping down the inside of the bowl occasionally.

4.   Scrape down and remove the beaters. Fold in the flour mixture and peanuts with a rubber spatula just until all the flour is moistened and the peanut bits are evenly distributed in the dough.

5.   For a small air fryer oven, coat the inside of a 6-inch round cake pan with baking spray. For a medium air fryer oven, coat the inside of a 7-inch round cake pan with baking spray. And for a large air fryer oven, coat the inside of an 8-inch round cake pan with baking spray. Scrape and gently press the dough into the prepared pan, spreading it into an even layer to the perimeter.

6.   Set the pan in the air fryer oven and air-fry undisturbed for 18 minutes, or until well browned.

7.   Transfer the pan to a wire rack and cool for 15 minutes. Loosen the cookie from the perimeter with a spatula, then invert the pan onto a cutting board and let the cookie come free. Remove the pan and reinvert the cookie onto the wire rack. Cool for 5 minutes more before slicing into wedges to serve.

Currant Carrot Cake

Servings: 6

Cooking Time: 30 Minutes

Ingredients:

- 1 cup unbleached flour
- 1 teaspoon baking powder
- 1 teaspoon baking soda
- ½ cup evaporated skim milk
- ½ cup brown sugar
- 2 tablespoons vegetable oil
- 1 egg
- 1 cup grated carrots
- ½ cup chopped currants
- ¼ cup finely chopped pecans
- Salt to taste
- Yogurt Cream Icing (recipe follows)

Directions:

1. Preheat the toaster oven to 350° F.

2. Combine all the ingredients in a medium bowl, stirring well to mix thoroughly.

3. Spread the batter in an oiled or nonstick 8½ × 8½ × 2-inch square baking (cake) pan.

4. BAKE for 30 minutes, or until a toothpick inserted in the center comes out clean. Cool on a wire rack. Ice with Yogurt Cream Icing.

Goat Cheese–stuffed Nectarines

Servings: 4

Cooking Time: 10 Minutes

Ingredients:

- 4 ripe nectarines, halved and pitted
- 1 tablespoon olive oil
- 1 cup soft goat cheese, room temperature
- 1 tablespoon maple syrup
- ¼ teaspoon vanilla extract
- ¼ teaspoon ground cinnamon
- 2 tablespoons pecans, chopped

Directions:

1. Preheat the toaster oven to 350°F on AIR FRY for 5 minutes.

2. Place the air-fryer basket in the baking tray and place the nectarines in the basket, hollow-side up. Brush the tops and hollow of the fruit with the olive oil.

3. In position 2, air fry for 5 minutes to soften and lightly brown the fruit.

4. While the fruit is air frying, in a small bowl, stir the goat cheese, maple syrup, vanilla, and cinnamon until well blended.

5. Take the fruit out and evenly divide the cheese filling between the halves. Air fry for 5 minutes until the filling is heated through and a little melted.

6. Serve topped with pecans.

Individual Peach Crisps

Servings: 2

Cooking Time: 60 Minutes

Ingredients:

- 2 tablespoons granulated sugar, divided
- 1 teaspoon lemon juice
- ¼ teaspoon cornstarch
- ⅛ teaspoon table salt, divided
- 1 pound frozen sliced peaches, thawed
- ⅓ cup whole almonds or pecans, chopped fine

- ¼ cup (1¼ ounces) all-purpose flour
- 2 tablespoons packed light brown sugar
- ⅛ teaspoon ground cinnamon
- Pinch ground nutmeg
- 3 tablespoons unsalted butter, melted and cooled

Directions:

1. Adjust toaster oven rack to lowest position and preheat the toaster oven to 425 degrees. Combine 1 tablespoon granulated sugar, lemon juice, cornstarch, and pinch salt in medium bowl. Gently toss peaches with sugar mixture and divide evenly between two 12-ounce ramekins.

2. Combine almonds, flour, brown sugar, cinnamon, nutmeg, remaining pinch salt, and remaining 1 tablespoon granulated sugar in now-empty bowl. Drizzle with melted butter and toss with fork until evenly moistened and mixture forms large chunks with some pea-size pieces throughout. Sprinkle topping evenly over peaches, breaking up any large chunks.

3. Place ramekins on aluminum foil–lined small rimmed baking sheet and bake until filling is bubbling around edges and topping is deep golden brown, 25 to 30 minutes, rotating sheet halfway through baking. Let crisps cool on wire rack for 15 minutes before serving.

Make-ahead Chocolate Chip Cookies

Servings: 12

Cooking Time: 45 Minutes

Ingredients:

- 2⅛ cups (10⅔ ounces) all-purpose flour
- ½ teaspoon baking soda
- ½ teaspoon table salt
- 1 cup packed (7 ounces) light brown sugar
- ½ cup (3½ ounces)granulated sugar
- 12 tablespoons unsalted butter, melted and cooled
- 1 large egg plus 1 large yolk
- 2 teaspoons vanilla extract
- 1 cup (6 ounces) semisweet chocolate chips

Directions:

1. Adjust toaster oven rack to middle position and preheat the toaster oven to 350 degrees. Line large and small rimmed baking sheets with parchment paper. Whisk flour, baking soda, and salt together in bowl.

2. Whisk brown sugar and granulated sugar together in medium bowl. Whisk in melted butter until combined. Whisk in egg and yolk and vanilla until smooth. Gently stir in flour mixture with rubber spatula until soft dough forms. Fold in chocolate chips.

3. Working with 2 tablespoons dough at a time, roll into balls. Space desired number of dough balls at least 1½ inches apart on prepared small sheet; space remaining dough balls evenly on prepared large sheet. Using bottom of greased dry measuring cup, press each ball until 2 inches in diameter.

4. Bake small sheet of cookies until edges are just beginning to brown and centers are soft and puffy, 10 to 15 minutes. Let cookies cool slightly on sheet. Serve warm or at room temperature.

5. Freeze remaining large sheet of cookies until firm, about 1 hour. Transfer cookies to 1-gallon zipper-lock bag and freeze for up to 1 month. Bake frozen cookies as directed; do not thaw.

Brown Sugar Baked Apples

Servings: 4

Cooking Time: 15 Minutes

Ingredients:

- 3 Small tart apples, preferably McIntosh
- 4 tablespoons (¼ cup/½ stick) Butter
- 6 tablespoons Light brown sugar
- Ground cinnamon
- Table salt

Directions:

1. Preheat the toaster oven to 400°F.

2. Stem the apples, then cut them in half through their "equators" (that is, not the stem ends). Use a melon baller to core the apples, taking care not to break through the flesh and skin at any point but creating a little well in the center of each half.

3. When the machine is at temperature, remove the baking pan and set it on a heat-safe work surface. Set the apple halves cut side up in the baking pan with as much air space between them as possible. Even a fraction of an inch will work. Drop 2 teaspoons of butter into the well in the center of each apple half. Sprinkle each half with 1 tablespoon brown sugar and a pinch each ground cinnamon and table salt.

4. Return the baking pan to the machine. Air-fry undisturbed for 15 minutes, or until the apple halves have softened and the brown sugar has caramelized.

5. Use a nonstick-safe spatula to transfer the apple halves cut side up to a wire rack. Cool for at least 10 minutes before serving, or serve at room temperature.

Scones

Servings: 8

Cooking Time: 20 Minutes

Ingredients:

- Scone mixture:
- 1 cup unbleached flour
- 1 teaspoon baking powder
- 2 ¼ cup brown sugar
- 3 tablespoons vegetable oil
- 4 ¼ cup low-fat buttermilk
- 5 ½ teaspoon vanilla extract
- Topping mixture:
- 1 tablespoon granulated sugar
- 1 tablespoon margarine
- 1 teaspoon ground cinnamon

Directions:

1. Preheat the toaster oven to 425° F.

2. Combine the scone mixture ingredients in a medium bowl, cutting to blend with 2 butter knives or a pastry blender. Add a little more buttermilk, if necessary, so that the dough is moist enough to stay together when pinched.

3. KNEAD the dough on a lightly floured surface for 2 minutes, then place the dough in an oiled or nonstick 9¾-inch round cake pan and pat

down to spread out evenly to the edges of the pan. Cut into 8 wedges.

4. Combine the topping mixture in a small bowl, mixing well, and sprinkle evenly on the dough.

5. BAKE for 20 minutes, or until golden brown.

Peach Cobbler

Servings: 4

Cooking Time: 35 Minutes

Ingredients:

- FOR THE FILLING
- 4 cups chopped fresh peaches
- ½ cup sugar
- 2 tablespoons cornstarch
- 1 teaspoon vanilla extract
- FOR THE COBBLER
- 1 cup all-purpose flour
- ¼ cup sugar
- ¾ teaspoon baking powder
- Pinch of sea salt
- 3 tablespoons cold salted butter, cut into ½-inch cubes
- ½ cup buttermilk

Directions:

1. To make the filling

2. In a medium bowl, toss together the peaches, sugar, cornstarch, and vanilla.

3. Transfer to an 8-inch-square baking dish. Set aside.

4. To make the cobbler

5. Place the rack in position 1 and preheat the toaster oven to 350°F on BAKE for 5 minutes.

6. In a large bowl, stir the flour, sugar, baking powder, and sea salt.

7. Using your fingertips, rub the butter into the flour mixture until the mixture resembles coarse crumbs.

8. Add the buttermilk in a thin stream to the flour crumbs, tossing with a fork until a sticky dough forms.

9. Scoop the batter by tablespoons and dollop it on the peaches, spacing the mounds out evenly and leaving gaps for the steam to escape.

10. Bake for 35 minutes, or until the cobbler is golden brown and the filling is bubbly.

11. Serve warm.

Keto Cheesecake Cups

Servings: 6

Cooking Time: 10 Minutes

Ingredients:

- 8 ounces cream cheese
- ¼ cup plain whole-milk Greek yogurt
- 1 large egg
- 1 teaspoon pure vanilla extract
- 3 tablespoons monk fruit sweetener
- ¼ teaspoon salt
- ½ cup walnuts, roughly chopped

Directions:

1. Preheat the toaster oven to 315°F.

2. In a large bowl, use a hand mixer to beat the cream cheese together with the yogurt, egg, vanilla, sweetener, and salt. When combined, fold in the chopped walnuts.

3. Set 6 silicone muffin liners inside an air-fryer-safe pan.

4. Evenly fill the cupcake liners with cheesecake batter.

5. Carefully place the pan into the air fryer oven and air-fry for about 10 minutes, or until the tops are lightly browned and firm.

6. Carefully remove the pan when done and place in the refrigerator for 3 hours to firm up before serving.

Lemon Torte

Servings: 6
Cooking Time: 16 Minutes

Ingredients:

- First mixture:
- ¼ cup margarine, at room temperature
- ½ teaspoon grated lemon zest
- 3 egg yolks
- ¼ cup sugar
- ⅓ cup unbleached flour
- 3 tablespoons cornstarch
- Second mixture:
- 3 egg whites
- 2 tablespoons sugar
- Cream Cheese Frosting (recipe follows)

Directions:

1. Beat together the first mixture ingredients in a medium bowl with an electric mixer until the mixture is smooth. Set aside. Clean the electric mixer beaters.

2. Beat the second mixture together: Beat the egg whites into soft peaks in a medium bowl, gradually adding the sugar, and continue beating until the peaks are stiff. Fold the first mixture into the second mixture to make the torte batter.

3. Pour ½ cup torte batter into a small oiled or nonstick 3½ × 7½ × 2¼-inch loaf pan.

4. BROIL for 1 or 2 minutes, or until lightly browned. Remove from the oven.

5. Pour and spread evenly another ½ cup batter on top of the first layer. Broil again for 1 or 2 minutes, or until lightly browned. Repeat the process until all the batter is used up. When cool, run a knife around the sides to loosen and invert onto a plate. Chill. Frost with Cream Cheese Frosting and serve chilled.

Soft Peanut Butter Cookies

Servings: 12
Cooking Time: 20 Minutes

Ingredients:

- 1/2 cup vegetable shortening
- 1/2 cup peanut butter
- 1 1/4 cups light brown sugar
- 1 egg
- 1 teaspoon vanilla
- 1/2 teaspoon salt
- 1 1/2 cups flour
- 1 teaspoon baking soda
- Sugar crystals

Directions:

1. Preheat the toaster oven to 275°F.

2. Using the flat beater attachment, beat shortening, peanut butter, brown sugar, egg, and vanilla at a medium setting until well blended.

3. Reduce speed to low and gradually add dry ingredients until blended. Dough will be crumbly.

4. Roll 3 tablespoon-size portions of the dough into a ball. Place on ungreased cookie sheet.

5. Press to 1/2-inch thick. Sprinkle with sugar crystals.

6. Bake 18 to 20 minutes. Do not overcook.

Carrot Cake

Servings: 6

Cooking Time: 30 Minutes

Ingredients:

- FOR THE CAKE
- ½ cup canola oil, plus extra for greasing the baking dish
- 1 cup all-purpose flour, plus extra for dusting the baking dish
- 1 cup granulated sugar
- 1 teaspoon baking powder
- ½ teaspoon sea salt
- 2 teaspoons pumpkin pie spice
- 2 large eggs
- 1 cup carrot, finely shredded
- ½ cup dried apricot, chopped
- FOR THE ICING
- 4 ounces cream cheese, room temperature
- ¼ cup salted butter, room temperature
- 1 teaspoon vanilla extract
- 2 cups confectioners' sugar

Directions:

1. To make the cake

2. Place the rack in position 1 and preheat the oven to 325°F on BAKE for 5 minutes.

3. Lightly grease an 8-inch-square baking dish with oil and dust with flour.

4. Place the rack in position 1.

5. In a large bowl, stir the flour, sugar, baking powder, salt, and pumpkin pie spice.

6. Make a well in the center and add the oil and eggs, stirring until just combined. Add the carrot and apricot and stir until well mixed.

7. Transfer the batter to the baking dish and bake for about 30 minutes until golden brown and a toothpick inserted in the center comes out clean.

8. Remove the cake from the oven and cool completely in the baking dish.

9. To make the icing

10. When the cake is cool, whisk the cream cheese, butter, and vanilla until very smooth and blended. Add the confectioners' sugar and whisk until creamy and thick, about 2 minutes.

11. Ice the cake and serve.

Campfire Banana Boats

Servings: 4

Cooking Time: 20 Minutes

Ingredients:

- 4 medium, unpeeled ripe bananas
- ¼ cup dark chocolate chips
- 4 teaspoons shredded, unsweetened coconut
- ½ cup mini marshmallows
- 4 graham crackers, chopped

Directions:

1. Preheat the toaster oven to 400°F on BAKE for 5 minutes.

2. Cut the bananas lengthwise through the skin about halfway through. Open the pocket to create a space for the other ingredients.

3. Evenly divide the chocolate, coconut, marshmallows, and graham crackers among the bananas.

4. Tear off four 12-inch squares of foil and place the bananas in the center of each. Crimp the foil around the banana to form a boat.

5. Place the bananas on the baking tray, two at a time, and in position 2, bake for 10 minutes until the fillings are gooey and the banana is warmed through.

6. Repeat with the remaining two bananas and serve.

Cinnamon Sugar Rolls

Servings: 8

Cooking Time: 10 Minutes

Ingredients:

- ½ cup margarine
- Filling mixture:
- 1 tablespoon ground cinnamon
- ½ cup brown sugar
- ½ cup finely chopped walnuts
- 10 sheets phyllo pastry, thawed

Directions:

1. BROIL the margarine in an oiled or nonstick 8½ × 8½ × 2-inch square baking (cake) pan for 3 minutes, or until almost melted. Remove from the oven and stir until melted (the pan will be hot and the margarine will continue to melt). Set aside.

2. Combine the filling mixture in a small bowl, mixing well.

3. Lay a sheet of phyllo pastry on a clean flat surface. Brush with the melted margarine, sprinkle with a heaping tablespoon of the filling mixture, and spread evenly to cover the sheet of pastry. Repeat the brushing and sprinkling procedure for each sheet, layering one on top of the other until all 10 sheets are done. Use up any remaining filling mixture on the last sheet. Starting at the 9-inch (long) edge, slowly roll all of the sheets up like a jelly roll. With a sharp knife, cut the roll into 1¼-inch slices. Place the slices on an oiled or nonstick baking sheet or baking pan.

4. BAKE at 350° F. for 10 minutes, or until golden brown.

Frozen Brazo De Mercedes

Servings: 8

Cooking Time: 15 Minutes

Ingredients:

- 1 pint vanilla ice cream, softened to room temperature
- 1 (8 inch) premade graham cracker crust
- 6 large eggs, yolks and whites separated
- 7 ounces condensed milk
- ½ teaspoon vanilla extract
- ¼ teaspoon cream of tartar
- ⅓ cup granulated sugar

Directions:

1. Spread the ice cream on the bottom of the graham cracker crust in an even layer, cover with

plastic wrap, and place in the freezer for 8 hours or overnight.

2. Whisk egg yolks and condensed milk over a double boiler continuously for 15 minutes or until the mixture becomes thick.

3. Whisk the vanilla extract into the egg mixture until fully combined.

4. Pass the custard through a fine sieve to remove any clumps.

5. Remove the ice cream and top with the egg yolk mixture, cover with plastic wrap, and place back into the freezer for 2 hours.

6. Beat the egg whites and cream of tartar in a stand mixer on high speed.

7. Add the sugar in slowly once the egg whites begin to foam.

8. Beat the egg whites for two minutes or until they form stiff peaks.

9. Remove the plastic wrap from the pie and top with the beaten egg whites.

10. Preheat the toaster Oven to 350°F.

11. Place the pie on the wire rack, then insert the rack at mid position in the preheated air fryer.

12. Select the Bake and Shake functions, adjust time to 15 minutes, and press Start/Pause.

13. Rotate the pie halfway through cooking for even browning. The Shake Reminder will let you know when.

14. Remove when done and place in the fridge for 1 hour, uncovered.

15. Cover the pie, then place in the freezer for 6 hours or overnight.

16. Remove the pie and allow it to rest at room temperature for 10 minutes, then slice and serve.

Coconut Rice Pudding

Servings: 6

Cooking Time: 55 Minutes

Ingredients:
- ½ cup short-grain brown rice
- Pudding mixture:
- 1 egg, beaten
- 1 tablespoon cornstarch
- ½ cup fat-free half-and-half
- ½ cup chopped raisins
- 1 teaspoon vanilla extract
- ½ teaspoon ground cinnamon
- ½ teaspoon grated nutmeg
- Salt to taste
- ¼ cup shredded sweetened coconut
- Fat-free whipped topping

Directions:
1. Preheat the toaster oven to 400° F.

2. Combine the rice and 1½ cups water in a 1-quart 8½ × 8½ × 4-inch ovenproof baking dish. Cover with aluminum foil.

3. BAKE, covered, for 45 minutes, or until the rice is tender. Remove from the oven and add the pudding mixture ingredients, mixing well.

4. BAKE, uncovered, for 10 minutes, or until the top is lightly browned. Sprinkle the top with coconut and chill before serving. Top with fat-free whipped topping.

Graham Cracker Crust

Servings: 4

Cooking Time: 14 Minutes

Ingredients:

- 1⅓ cups reduced-fat graham cracker crumbs
- 2 tablespoons brown sugar
- 1 teaspoon ground cinnamon
- Salt to taste
- 1 tablespoon margarine
- 2 tablespoons vegetable oil

Directions:

1. Process the graham crackers in a food processor or blender to produce finely ground crumbs. Add the sugar, cinnamon, and salt and blend by stirring. Set aside.

2. Heat the margarine and oil under a broiler for 4 minutes, or until the margarine is almost melted. Remove from the oven and stir until the margarine is completely melted. Add the graham cracker crumbs and mix thoroughly.

3. Press the mixture into a 9¾-inch pie pan, spreading it out evenly from the middle and up the sides of the pan.

4. BAKE at 350° F. for 10 minutes, or until lightly browned. Cool before filling.

Sweet Potato Donut Holes

Servings: 18

Cooking Time: 4 Minutes

Ingredients:

- 1 cup flour
- ⅓ cup sugar
- ¼ teaspoon baking soda
- 1 teaspoon baking powder
- ⅛ teaspoon salt
- ½ cup cooked mashed purple sweet potatoes
- 1 egg, beaten
- 2 tablespoons butter, melted
- 1 teaspoon pure vanilla extract
- oil for misting or cooking spray

Directions:

1. Preheat the toaster oven to 390°F.

2. In a large bowl, stir together the flour, sugar, baking soda, baking powder, and salt.

3. In a separate bowl, combine the potatoes, egg, butter, and vanilla and mix well.

4. Add potato mixture to dry ingredients and stir into a soft dough.

5. Shape dough into 1½-inch balls. Mist lightly with oil or cooking spray.

6. Place 9 donut holes in air fryer oven, leaving a little space in between. Air-fry for 4 minutes, until done in center and lightly browned outside.

7. Repeat step 6 to cook remaining donut holes.

Fried Snickers Bars

Servings: 8

Cooking Time: 4 Minutes

Ingredients:

- ⅓ cup All-purpose flour
- 1 Large egg white(s), beaten until foamy
- 1½ cups (6 ounces) Vanilla wafer cookie crumbs
- 8 Fun-size (0.6-ounce/17-gram) Snickers bars, frozen

- Vegetable oil spray

Directions:

1. Preheat the toaster oven to 400°F.

2. Set up and fill three shallow soup plates or small pie plates on your counter: one for the flour, one for the beaten egg white(s), and one for the cookie crumbs.

3. Unwrap the frozen candy bars. Dip one in the flour, turning it to coat on all sides. Gently stir any excess, then set it in the beaten egg white(s). Turn it to coat all sides, even the ends, then let any excess egg white slip back into the rest. Set the candy bar in the cookie crumbs. Turn to coat on all sides, even the ends. Dip the candy bar back in the egg white(s) a second time, then into the cookie crumbs a second time, making sure you have an even coating all around. Coat the covered candy bar all over with vegetable oil spray. Set aside so you can dip and coat the remaining candy bars.

4. Set the coated candy bars in the pan with as much air space between them as possible. Air-fry undisturbed for 4 minutes, or until golden brown.

5. Remove the pan from the machine and let the candy bars cool in the pan for 10 minutes. Use a nonstick-safe spatula to transfer them to a wire rack and cool for 5 minutes more before chowing down.

VEGETABLES AND VEGETARIAN

Zucchini Boats With Ham And Cheese

Servings: 4

Cooking Time: 12 Minutes

Ingredients:

- 2 6-inch-long zucchini
- 2 ounces Thinly sliced deli ham, any rind removed, meat roughly chopped
- 4 Dry-packed sun-dried tomatoes, chopped
- ⅓ cup Purchased pesto
- ¼ cup Packaged mini croutons
- ¼ cup (about 1 ounce) Shredded semi-firm mozzarella cheese

Directions:

1. Preheat the toaster oven to 375°F .

2. Split the zucchini in half lengthwise and use a flatware spoon or a serrated grapefruit spoon to scoop out the insides of the halves, leaving at least a ¼-inch border all around the zucchini half. (You can save the scooped out insides to add to soups and stews—or even freeze it for a much later use.)

3. Mix the ham, sun-dried tomatoes, pesto, croutons, and half the cheese in a bowl until well combined. Pack this mixture into the zucchini "shells." Top them with the remaining cheese.

4. Set them stuffing side up in the air fryer oven without touching (even a fraction of an inch between them is enough room). Air-fry undisturbed for 12 minutes, or until softened and browned, with the cheese melted on top.

5. Use a nonstick-safe spatula to transfer the zucchini boats stuffing side up on a wire rack. Cool for 5 or 10 minutes before serving.

Roasted Garlic Potatoes

Servings: 2

Cooking Time: 40 Minutes

Ingredients:

- 2 medium potatoes, peeled and chopped
- 6 garlic cloves, roasted
- 1 tablespoon olive oil
- Salt and freshly ground black pepper
- 1 tablespoon chopped fresh parsley

Directions:

1. Preheat the toaster oven to 400° F.

2. Place the potatoes in an oiled or nonstick 8½ × 8½ × 2-inch square baking (cake) pan. Add the garlic, oil, and salt and pepper to taste. Toss to coat well. Cover the pan with aluminum foil.

3. BAKE, covered, for 40 minutes, or until the potatoes are tender. Remove the cover.

4. BROIL 10 minutes, or until lightly browned. Garnish with fresh parsley before serving.

Fried Cauliflower with Parmesan Lemon Dressing

Servings: 2

Cooking Time: 12 Minutes

Ingredients:

- 4 cups cauliflower florets (about half a large head)
- 1 tablespoon olive oil
- salt and freshly ground black pepper
- 1 teaspoon finely chopped lemon zest
- 1 tablespoon fresh lemon juice (about half a lemon)
- ¼ cup grated Parmigiano-Reggiano cheese
- 4 tablespoons extra virgin olive oil
- ¼ teaspoon salt
- lots of freshly ground black pepper
- 1 tablespoon chopped fresh parsley

Directions:

1. Preheat the toaster oven to 400°F.

2. Toss the cauliflower florets with the olive oil, salt and freshly ground black pepper. Air-fry for 12 minutes.

3. While the cauliflower is frying, make the dressing. Combine the lemon zest, lemon juice, Parmigiano-Reggiano cheese and olive oil in a small bowl. Season with salt and lots of freshly ground black pepper. Stir in the parsley.

4. Turn the fried cauliflower out onto a serving platter and drizzle the dressing over the top.

Sesame Carrots And Sugar Snap Peas

Servings: 16

Cooking Time: 4 Minutes

Ingredients:

- 1 pound carrots, peeled sliced on the bias (½-inch slices)
- 1 teaspoon olive oil
- salt and freshly ground black pepper
- ⅓ cup honey
- 1 tablespoon sesame oil
- 1 tablespoon soy sauce
- ½ teaspoon minced fresh ginger
- 4 ounces sugar snap peas (about 1 cup)
- 1½ teaspoons sesame seeds

Directions:

1. Preheat the toaster oven to 360°F.

2. Toss the carrots with the olive oil, season with salt and pepper and air-fry for 10 minutes.

3. Combine the honey, sesame oil, soy sauce and minced ginger in a large bowl. Add the sugar snap peas and the air-fried carrots to the honey mixture, toss to coat and return everything to the air fryer oven.

4. Turn up the temperature to 400°F and air-fry for an additional 6 minutes.

5. Transfer the carrots and sugar snap peas to a serving bowl. Pour the sauce from the bottom of the cooker over the vegetables and sprinkle sesame seeds over top. Serve immediately.

Roasted Ratatouille Vegetables

Servings: 15

Cooking Time: 2 Minutes

Ingredients:

- 1 baby or Japanese eggplant, cut into 1½-inch cubes
- 1 red pepper, cut into 1-inch chunks
- 1 yellow pepper, cut into 1-inch chunks
- 1 zucchini, cut into 1-inch chunks
- 1 clove garlic, minced
- ½ teaspoon dried basil
- 1 tablespoon olive oil
- salt and freshly ground black pepper
- ¼ cup sliced sun-dried tomatoes in oil
- 2 tablespoons chopped fresh basil

Directions:

1. Preheat the toaster oven to 400°F.

2. Toss the eggplant, peppers and zucchini with the garlic, dried basil, olive oil, salt and freshly ground black pepper.

3. Air-fry the vegetables at 400°F for 15 minutes.

4. As soon as the vegetables are tender, toss them with the sliced sun-dried tomatoes and fresh basil and serve.

Roasted Herbed Shiitake Mushrooms

Servings: 5

Cooking Time: 4 Minutes

Ingredients:

- 8 ounces shiitake mushrooms, stems removed and caps roughly chopped
- 1 tablespoon olive oil
- ½ teaspoon salt
- freshly ground black pepper
- 1 teaspoon chopped fresh thyme leaves
- 1 teaspoon chopped fresh oregano
- 1 tablespoon chopped fresh parsley

Directions:

1. Preheat the toaster oven to 400°F.

2. Toss the mushrooms with the olive oil, salt, pepper, thyme and oregano. Air-fry for 5 minutes. The mushrooms will still be somewhat chewy with a meaty texture. If you'd like them a little more tender, add a couple of minutes to this cooking time.

3. Once cooked, add the parsley to the mushrooms and toss. Season again to taste and serve.

Roasted Heirloom Carrots With Orange And Thyme

Servings: 2

Cooking Time: 12 Minutes

Ingredients:

- 10 to 12 heirloom or rainbow carrots (about 1 pound), scrubbed but not peeled
- 1 teaspoon olive oil
- salt and freshly ground black pepper
- 1 tablespoon butter
- 1 teaspoon fresh orange zest
- 1 teaspoon chopped fresh thyme

Directions:

1. Preheat the toaster oven to 400°F.

2.   Scrub the carrots and halve them lengthwise. Toss them in the olive oil, season with salt and freshly ground black pepper and transfer to the air fryer oven.

3.   Air-fry at 400°F for 12 minutes.

4.   As soon as the carrots have finished cooking, add the butter, orange zest and thyme and toss all the ingredients together in the air fryer oven to melt the butter and coat evenly. Serve warm.

Rolled Chinese (napa) Cabbage With Chickpea Filling

Servings: 4

Cooking Time: 46 Minutes

Ingredients:

- 6 Chinese cabbage leaves, approximately 7 inches long
- Filling:
- 2 tablespoons low-fat ricotta cheese or Yogurt Cheese Spread
- 1 cup canned chickpeas (garbanzos), drained and mashed
- 1 teaspoon lemon juice
- Salt and butcher's pepper to taste
- 2 tablespoons olive oil for brushing
- 2 tablespoons chopped almonds

Directions:

1.   Layer an 8½ × 8½ × 2-inch square baking (cake) pan with the cabbage leaves and add enough water to barely cover them.

2.   BROIL 5 minutes, turn the leaves with tongs, and broil another 5 minutes, or until the leaves are partially cooked and just pliable. Spread the leaves on paper towels to drain and cool.

3.   Mix the filling ingredients together in a medium bowl and adjust the seasonings to taste. Place equal portions of filling 2 inches from the stem end (base of the leaf) and roll up the leaf, enclosing the filling. Place each roll with the leaf edge down in an oiled or 8½ × 8½ × 2-inch square baking (cake) pan. Sprinkle with the almonds. Cover the pan with aluminum foil.

4.   BAKE at 400° F. for 30 minutes, or until the rolls are tender. Remove the cover.

5.   BROIL 6 minutes, or until the almonds and cabbage leaves are lightly browned.

Lentil-stuffed Zucchini

Servings: 2

Cooking Time: 50 Minutes

Ingredients:

- 2 large zucchini
- 2 teaspoons olive oil
- 1 (15-ounce) can low-sodium lentils, drained and rinsed
- 1 large tomato, chopped
- 1 scallion, both white and green parts, chopped
- ½ jalapeño pepper, minced
- ½ cup corn kernels, fresh or frozen (thawed)
- 1 tablespoon fresh cilantro, chopped
- 1 teaspoon minced garlic
- 1 teaspoon ground cumin
- ¼ teaspoon chili powder
- ½ cup shredded Monterey Jack cheese

Directions:

1. Preheat the toaster oven to 400°F on BAKE for 5 minutes.

2. Line the baking tray with parchment paper.

3. Cut the zucchini in half lengthwise and scoop out the insides so that you have a hollow shell (about ¼-inch thick all the way around).

4. Lightly oil both sides of the zucchini shells and set them on the baking sheet.

5. In a large bowl, stir the lentils, tomato, scallion, jalapeño, corn, cilantro, garlic, cumin, and chili powder until well mixed.

6. Spoon the lentil mixture into the zucchini and top with the cheese.

7. Bake for 50 minutes. The zucchini should be tender, the filling heated through, and the cheese melted and lightly browned. Serve.

Steakhouse Baked Potatoes

Servings: 3

Cooking Time: 55 Minutes

Ingredients:

- 3 10-ounce russet potatoes
- 2 tablespoons Olive oil
- 1 teaspoon Table salt

Directions:

1. Preheat the toaster oven to 375°F .

2. Poke holes all over each potato with a fork. Rub the skin of each potato with 2 teaspoons of the olive oil, then sprinkle ¼ teaspoon salt all over each potato.

3. When the machine is at temperature, set the potatoes in the air fryer oven in one layer with as much air space between them as possible. Air-fry for 50 minutes, turning once, or until soft to the touch but with crunchy skins. If the machine is at 360°F, you may need to add up to 5 minutes to the cooking time.

4. Use kitchen tongs to gently transfer the baked potatoes to a wire rack. Cool for 5 or 10 minutes before serving.

Grits Casserole

Servings: 4

Cooking Time: 30 Minutes

Ingredients:

- 10 fresh asparagus spears, cut into 1-inch pieces
- 2 cups cooked grits, cooled to room temperature
- 1 egg, beaten
- 2 teaspoons Worcestershire sauce
- ½ teaspoon garlic powder
- ¼ teaspoon salt
- 2 slices provolone cheese (about 1½ ounces)
- oil for misting or cooking spray

Directions:

1. Mist asparagus spears with oil and air-fry at 390°F for 5 minutes, until crisp-tender.

2. In a medium bowl, mix together the grits, egg, Worcestershire, garlic powder, and salt.

3. Spoon half of grits mixture into air fryer oven baking pan and top with asparagus.

4. Tear cheese slices into pieces and layer evenly on top of asparagus.

5. Top with remaining grits.

6. Bake at 360°F for 25 minutes. The casserole will rise a little as it cooks. When done, the top will have browned lightly with just a hint of crispiness.

Classic Baked Potatoes

Servings: 4

Cooking Time: 50 Minutes

Ingredients:

- 4 medium baking potatoes,
- scrubbed and pierced with a fork

Directions:

1. Preheat the toaster oven to 450° F.

2. BAKE the potatoes on the oven rack for 50 minutes, or until tender when pierced with a fork.

Roasted Root Vegetables With Cinnamon

Servings: 4

Cooking Time: 20 Minutes

Ingredients:

- 1 small sweet potato, cut into 1-inch pieces
- 2 carrots, cut into 1-inch pieces
- 2 parsnips, cut into 1-inch pieces
- 2 tablespoons brown sugar (dark or light)
- 1 tablespoon olive oil
- ¼ teaspoon ground cinnamon
- Oil spray (hand-pumped)
- Sea salt, for seasoning

Directions:

1. Preheat the toaster oven to 350°F on AIR FRY for 5 minutes.

2. In a large bowl, toss the sweet potato, carrots, parsnips, brown sugar, oil, and cinnamon until well mixed.

3. Place the air-fryer basket in the baking tray and generously spray the mesh with oil.

4. Spread the vegetables in the basket and air fry in position 2 for 20 minutes, shaking the basket after 10 minutes, until the vegetables are tender and lightly caramelized.

5. Season with salt and serve.

Roasted Belgian Endive With Pistachios And Lemon

Servings: 2

Cooking Time: 7 Minutes

Ingredients:

- 2 Medium 3-ounce Belgian endive head(s)
- 2 tablespoons Olive oil
- ½ teaspoon Table salt
- ¼ cup Finely chopped unsalted shelled pistachios
- Up to 2 teaspoons Lemon juice

Directions:

1. Preheat the toaster oven to 325°F (or 330°F, if that's the closest setting).

2. Trim the Belgian endive head(s), removing the little bit of dried-out stem end but keeping the leaves intact. Quarter the head(s) through the stem (which will hold the leaves intact). Brush the endive quarters with oil, getting it down between the leaves. Sprinkle the quarters with salt.

3. When the machine is at temperature, set the endive quarters cut sides up in the air fryer oven

with as much air space between them as possible. They should not touch. Air-fry undisturbed for 7 minutes, or until lightly browned along the edges.

4. Use kitchen tongs to transfer the endive quarters to serving plates or a platter. Sprinkle with the pistachios and lemon juice. Serve warm or at room temperature.

Baked Mac And Cheese

Servings: 4
Cooking Time: 45 Minutes

Ingredients:

- Oil spray (hand-pumped)
- 1½ cups whole milk, room temperature
- ½ cup heavy (whipping) cream, room temperature
- 1 cup shredded cheddar cheese
- 4 ounces cream cheese, room temperature
- ½ teaspoon dry mustard
- ⅛ teaspoon sea salt
- ⅛ teaspoon freshly ground black pepper
- 1¼ cups dried elbow macaroni
- ¼ cup bread crumbs
- 2 tablespoons grated Parmesan cheese
- 1 tablespoon salted butter, melted

Directions:

1. Place the rack in position 1 and preheat the toaster oven to 375°F on CONVECTION BAKE for 5 minutes.

2. Lightly coat an 8-inch-square baking dish with the oil spray.

3. In a large bowl, stir the milk, cream, cheddar, cream cheese, mustard, salt, and pepper until well combined.

4. Transfer the mixture to the baking dish, stir in the macaroni and cover tightly with foil.

5. Bake for 35 minutes.

6. While the macaroni is baking, in a small bowl, stir the bread crumbs, Parmesan, and butter to form coarse crumbs. Set aside.

7. Take the baking dish out of the oven, uncover, stir, and evenly cover with the bread crumb mixture.

8. Bake uncovered for an additional 10 minutes until the pasta is tender, bubbly, and golden brown. Serve.

Perfect Asparagus

Servings: 3
Cooking Time: 10 Minutes

Ingredients:

- 1 pound Very thin asparagus spears
- 2 tablespoons Olive oil
- 1 teaspoon Coarse sea salt or kosher salt
- ¾ teaspoon Finely grated lemon zest

Directions:

1. Preheat the toaster oven to 400°F.

2. Trim just enough off the bottom of the asparagus spears so they'll fit in the air fryer oven. Put the spears on a large plate and drizzle them with some of the olive oil. Turn them over and drizzle more olive oil, working to get all the spears coated.

3. When the machine is at temperature, place the spears in one direction in the air fryer oven. They may be touching. Air-fry for 10 minutes, tossing and rearranging the spears twice, until tender.

4. Dump the contents of the air fryer oven on a serving platter. Spread out the spears. Sprinkle them with the salt and lemon zest while still warm. Serve at once.

Asparagus Fries

Servings: 4

Cooking Time: 5 Minutes

Ingredients:

- 12 ounces fresh asparagus spears with tough ends trimmed off
- 2 egg whites
- ¼ cup water
- ¾ cup panko breadcrumbs
- ¼ cup grated Parmesan cheese, plus 2 tablespoons
- ¼ teaspoon salt
- oil for misting or cooking spray

Directions:

1. Preheat the toaster oven to 390°F.

2. In a shallow dish, beat egg whites and water until slightly foamy.

3. In another shallow dish, combine panko, Parmesan, and salt.

4. Dip asparagus spears in egg, then roll in crumbs. Spray with oil or cooking spray.

5. Place a layer of asparagus in air fryer oven, leaving just a little space in between each spear.

Stack another layer on top, crosswise. Air-fry at 390°F for 5 minutes, until crispy and golden brown.

6. Repeat to cook remaining asparagus.

Salt And Pepper Baked Potatoes

Servings: 40

Cooking Time: 4 Minutes

Ingredients:

- 1 to 2 tablespoons olive oil
- 4 medium russet potatoes (about 9 to 10 ounces each)
- salt and coarsely ground black pepper
- butter, sour cream, chopped fresh chives, scallions or bacon bits (optional)

Directions:

1. Preheat the toaster oven to 400°F.

2. Rub the olive oil all over the potatoes and season them generously with salt and coarsely ground black pepper. Pierce all sides of the potatoes several times with the tines of a fork.

3. Air-fry for 40 minutes, turning the potatoes over halfway through the cooking time.

4. Serve the potatoes, split open with butter, sour cream, fresh chives, scallions or bacon bits.

Tandoori Cauliflower

Servings: 4

Cooking Time: 10 Minutes

Ingredients:

- ½ cup Plain full-fat yogurt (not Greek yogurt)
- 1½ teaspoons Yellow curry powder, purchased or homemade

- 1½ teaspoons Lemon juice
- ¾ teaspoon Table salt (optional)
- 4½ cups (about 1 pound 2 ounces) 2-inch cauliflower florets

Directions:

1. Preheat the toaster oven to 400°F.

2. Whisk the yogurt, curry powder, lemon juice, and salt (if using) in a large bowl until uniform. Add the florets and stir gently to coat the florets well and evenly. Even better, use your clean, dry hands to get the yogurt mixture down into all the nooks of the florets.

3. When the machine is at temperature, transfer the florets to the air fryer oven, spreading them gently into as close to one layer as you can. Air-fry for 10 minutes, tossing and rearranging the florets twice so that any covered or touching parts are exposed to the air currents, until lightly browned and tender if still a bit crunchy.

4. Pour the contents of the air fryer oven onto a wire rack. Cool for at least 5 minutes before serving, or serve at room temperature.

Potatoes Au Gratin

Servings: 4
Cooking Time: 40 Minutes

Ingredients:

- Mixture:
- ½ cup fat-free half-and-half
- ¼ cup nonfat plain yogurt
- 2 tablespoons margarine
- 2 tablespoons unbleached flour
- 1 teaspoon garlic powder

- ¼ cup shredded low-fat mozzarella cheese
- 2 tablespoons grated Parmesan cheese
- Salt and butcher's pepper to taste
- 2 cups peeled and diced potatoes
- ½ cup chopped onion
- 1 tablespoon fresh or frozen chives
- ¼ teaspoon paprika

Directions:

1. Preheat the toaster oven to 400° F.

2. Process the mixture ingredients in a food processor or blender until smooth. Pour into a 1-quart 8½ × 8½ × 4-inch ovenproof baking dish.

3. Add the potatoes, onion, chives, and paprika and stir to mix well. Cover the dish with aluminum foil.

4. BAKE, covered, for 40 minutes, or until the potatoes and onion are tender.

Grits Again

Servings: 2
Cooking Time: 10 Minutes

Ingredients:

- cooked grits
- plain breadcrumbs
- oil for misting or cooking spray
- honey or maple syrup for serving (optional)

Directions:

1. While grits are still warm, spread them into a square or rectangular baking pan, about ½-inch thick. If your grits are thicker than that, scoop some out into another pan.

2. Chill several hours or overnight, until grits are cold and firm.

3. When ready to cook, pour off any water that has collected in pan and cut grits into 2- to 3-inch squares.

4. Dip grits squares in breadcrumbs and place in air fryer oven in single layer, close but not touching.

5. Air-fry at 390°F for 10 minutes, until heated through and crispy brown on the outside.

6. Serve while hot either plain or with a drizzle of honey or maple syrup.

Brown Rice And Goat Cheese Croquettes

Servings: 3

Cooking Time: 8 Minutes

Ingredients:

- ¾ cup Water
- 6 tablespoons Raw medium-grain brown rice, such as brown Arborio
- ½ cup Shredded carrot
- ¼ cup Walnut pieces
- 3 tablespoons (about 1½ ounces) Soft goat cheese
- 1 tablespoon Pasteurized egg substitute, such as Egg Beaters (gluten-free, if a concern)
- ¼ teaspoon Dried thyme
- ¼ teaspoon Table salt
- ¼ teaspoon Ground black pepper
- Olive oil spray

Directions:

1. Combine the water, rice, and carrots in a small saucepan set over medium-high heat. Bring to a boil, stirring occasionally. Cover, reduce the heat to very low, and simmer very slowly for 45 minutes, or until the water has been absorbed and the rice is tender. Set aside, covered, for 10 minutes.

2. Scrape the contents of the saucepan into a food processor. Cool for 10 minutes.

3. Preheat the toaster oven to 400°F.

4. Put the nuts, cheese, egg substitute, thyme, salt, and pepper into the food processor. Cover and pulse to a coarse paste, stopping the machine at least once to scrape down the inside of the canister.

5. Uncover the food processor; scrape down and remove the blade. Using wet, clean hands, form the mixture into two 4-inch-diameter patties for a small batch, three 4-inch-diameter patties for a medium batch, or four 4-inch-diameter patties for a large one. Generously coat both sides of the patties with olive oil spray.

6. Set the patties in the air fryer oven with as much air space between them as possible. Air-fry undisturbed for 8 minutes, or until brown and crisp.

7. Use a nonstick-safe spatula to transfer the croquettes to a wire rack. Cool for 5 minutes before serving.

Simply Sweet Potatoes

Servings: 2

Cooking Time: 35 Minutes

Ingredients:

- 2 medium sweet potatoes, scrubbed and slit on top
- ¼ teaspoon ground thyme per potato

- 1 tablespoon lemon juice per potato
- ½ teaspoon margarine per potato
- Salt and freshly ground black pepper

Directions:

1. Preheat the toaster oven to 425° F.

2. BAKE the potatoes on the oven rack for 35 minutes, or until tender.

3. Open the slit and fluff the sweet potato pulp with a fork. Sprinkle the pulp with equal portions of thyme, lemon juice, and margarine. Fluff again. Season with salt and pepper to taste.

Roasted Corn Salad

Servings: 3
Cooking Time: 15 Minutes

Ingredients:

- 3 4-inch lengths husked and de-silked corn on the cob
- Olive oil spray
- 1 cup Packed baby arugula leaves
- 12 Cherry tomatoes, halved
- Up to 3 Medium scallion(s), trimmed and thinly sliced
- 2 tablespoons Lemon juice
- 1 tablespoon Olive oil
- 1½ teaspoons Honey
- ¼ teaspoon Mild paprika
- ¼ teaspoon Dried oregano
- ¼ teaspoon, plus more to taste Table salt
- ¼ teaspoon Ground black pepper

Directions:

1. Preheat the toaster oven to 400°F.

2. When the machine is at temperature, lightly coat the pieces of corn on the cob with olive oil spray. Set the pieces of corn in the air fryer oven with as much air space between them as possible. Air-fry undisturbed for 15 minutes, or until the corn is charred in a few spots.

3. Use kitchen tongs to transfer the corn to a wire rack. Cool for 15 minutes.

4. Cut the kernels off the ears by cutting the fat end off each piece so it will stand up straight on a cutting board, then running a knife down the corn. (Or you can save your fingers and buy a fancy tool to remove kernels from corn cobs. Check it out at online kitchenware stores.) Scoop the kernels into a serving bowl.

5. Chop the arugula into bite-size bits and add these to the kernels. Add the tomatoes and scallions, too. Whisk the lemon juice, olive oil, honey, paprika, oregano, salt, and pepper in a small bowl until the honey dissolves. Pour over the salad and toss well to coat, tasting for extra salt before serving.

Mushrooms, Sautéed

Servings: 4
Cooking Time: 4 Minutes

Ingredients:

- 8 ounces sliced white mushrooms, rinsed and well drained
- ¼ teaspoon garlic powder
- 1 tablespoon Worcestershire sauce

Directions:

1. Place mushrooms in a large bowl and sprinkle with garlic powder and Worcestershire. Stir well to distribute seasonings evenly.

2. Place in air fryer oven and air-fry at 390°F for 4 minutes, until tender.

BEEF PORK AND LAMB

Meatloaf With Tangy Tomato Glaze

Servings: 6
Cooking Time: 50 Minutes

Ingredients:

- 1 pound ground beef
- ½ pound ground pork
- ½ pound ground veal (or turkey)
- 1 medium onion, diced
- 1 small clove of garlic, minced
- 2 egg yolks, lightly beaten
- ½ cup tomato ketchup
- 1 tablespoon Worcestershire sauce
- ½ cup plain breadcrumbs
- 2 teaspoons salt
- freshly ground black pepper
- ½ cup chopped fresh parsley, plus more for garnish
- 6 tablespoons ketchup
- 1 tablespoon balsamic vinegar
- 2 tablespoons brown sugar

Directions:

1. Combine the meats, onion, garlic, egg yolks, ketchup, Worcestershire sauce, breadcrumbs, salt, pepper and fresh parsley in a large bowl and mix well.

2. Preheat the toaster oven to 350°F and pour a little water into the bottom of the air fryer oven. (This will help prevent the grease that drips into the bottom drawer from burning and smoking.)

3. Transfer the meatloaf mixture to the air fryer oven, packing it down gently. Run a spatula around the meatloaf to create a space about ½-inch wide between the meat and the side of the air fryer oven.

4. Air-fry at 350°F for 20 minutes. Carefully invert the meatloaf onto a plate (remember to remove the pan from the air fryer oven so you don't pour all the grease out) and slide it back into the air fryer oven to turn it over. Re-shape the meatloaf with a spatula if necessary. Air-fry for another 20 minutes at 350°F.

5. Combine the ketchup, balsamic vinegar and brown sugar in a bowl and spread the mixture over the meatloaf. Air-fry for another 10 minutes, until an instant read thermometer inserted into the center of the meatloaf registers 160°F.

6. Allow the meatloaf to rest for a few more minutes and then transfer it to a serving platter using a spatula. Slice the meatloaf, sprinkle a little chopped parsley on top if desired, and serve.

Smokehouse-style Beef Ribs

Servings: 3
Cooking Time: 25 Minutes

Ingredients:

- ¼ teaspoon Mild smoked paprika
- ¼ teaspoon Garlic powder
- ¼ teaspoon Onion powder

- ¼ teaspoon Table salt
- ¼ teaspoon Ground black pepper
- 3 10- to 12-ounce beef back ribs (not beef short ribs)

Directions:

1. Preheat the toaster oven to 350°F .

2. Mix the smoked paprika, garlic powder, onion powder, salt, and pepper in a small bowl until uniform. Massage and pat this mixture onto the ribs.

3. When the machine is at temperature, set the ribs in the air fryer oven in one layer, turning them on their sides if necessary, sort of like they're spooning but with at least ¼ inch air space between them. Air-fry for 25 minutes, turning once, until deep brown and sizzling.

4. Use kitchen tongs to transfer the ribs to a wire rack. Cool for 5 minutes before serving.

Skirt Steak Fajitas

Servings: 4
Cooking Time: 30 Minutes

Ingredients:

- 2 tablespoons olive oil
- ¼ cup lime juice
- 1 clove garlic, minced
- ½ teaspoon ground cumin
- ½ teaspoon hot sauce
- ½ teaspoon salt
- 2 tablespoons chopped fresh cilantro
- 1 pound skirt steak
- 1 onion, sliced
- 1 teaspoon chili powder
- 1 red pepper, sliced
- 1 green pepper, sliced
- salt and freshly ground black pepper
- 8 flour tortillas
- shredded lettuce, crumbled Queso Fresco (or grated Cheddar cheese), sliced black olives, diced tomatoes, sour cream and guacamole for serving

Directions:

1. Combine the olive oil, lime juice, garlic, cumin, hot sauce, salt and cilantro in a shallow dish. Add the skirt steak and turn it over several times to coat all sides. Pierce the steak with a needle-style meat tenderizer or paring knife. Marinate the steak in the refrigerator for at least 3 hours, or overnight. When you are ready to cook, remove the steak from the refrigerator and let it sit at room temperature for 30 minutes.

2. Preheat the toaster oven to 400°F.

3. Toss the onion slices with the chili powder and a little olive oil and transfer them to the air fryer oven. Air-fry at 400°F for 5 minutes. Add the red and green peppers to the air fryer oven with the onions, season with salt and pepper and air-fry for 8 more minutes, until the onions and peppers are soft. Transfer the vegetables to a dish and cover with aluminum foil to keep warm.

4. Place the skirt steak in the air fryer oven and pour the marinade over the top. Air-fry at 400°F for 12 minutes. Flip the steak over and air-fry at 400°F for an additional 5 minutes. (The time needed for your steak will depend on the thickness of the skirt steak. 17 minutes should bring your steak to roughly medium.) Transfer

the cooked steak to a cutting board and let the steak rest for a few minutes. If the peppers and onions need to be heated, return them to the air fryer oven for just 1 to 2 minutes.

5. Thinly slice the steak at an angle, cutting against the grain of the steak. Serve the steak with the onions and peppers, the warm tortillas and the fajita toppings on the side so that everyone can make their own fajita.

Herbed Lamb Burgers

Servings: 4
Cooking Time: 15 Minutes

Ingredients:
- 1 pound lean ground lamb
- 1 large egg
- 1 tablespoon fresh parsley, chopped
- 2 teaspoons fresh mint, chopped
- 1 teaspoon minced garlic
- ¼ teaspoon sea salt
- ⅛ teaspoon freshly ground black pepper
- Olive oil spray (hand-pumped)
- 4 whole-wheat buns
- ¼ cup store-bought tzatziki sauce
- 1 tomato, cut into slices
- 4 thin red onion slices
- ½ cup shredded lettuce

Directions:
1. Preheat the toaster oven to 350°F on CONVECTION BROIL for 5 minutes.
2. In a large bowl, mix the lamb, egg, parsley, mint, garlic, salt, and pepper. Form the mixture into 4 patties.
3. Place the air-fryer basket in the baking tray and place the burger patties in the basket. Lightly spray the patties with the oil on both sides.

4. In position 2, broil for 15 minutes, turning halfway through.
5. Serve on the buns topped with tzatziki sauce, tomato, onion, and lettuce.

Classic Pepperoni Pizza

Servings: 4
Cooking Time: 11 Minutes

Ingredients:
- Oil spray (hand-pumped)
- 1 pound premade pizza dough, or your favorite recipe
- ½ cup store-bought pizza sauce
- ¼ cup grated Parmesan cheese
- ¾ cup shredded mozzarella
- 10 to 12 slices pepperoni
- 2 tablespoons chopped fresh basil
- Pinch red pepper flakes

Directions:
1. Preheat the toaster oven to 425°F on BAKE for 5 minutes.
2. Spray the baking tray with the oil and spread the pizza dough with your fingertips so that it covers the tray. Prick the dough with a fork.
3. In position 2, bake for 8 minutes until the crust is lightly golden.
4. Take the crust out and spread with the pizza sauce, leaving a ½-inch border around the edge. Sprinkle with Parmesan and mozzarella cheeses and arrange the pepperoni on the pizza.
5. Bake for 3 minutes until the cheese is melted and bubbly.
6. Top with the basil and red pepper flakes and serve.

Spicy Flank Steak With Fresh Tomato-corn Salsa

Servings: 4

Cooking Time: 20 Minutes

Ingredients:

- 2 large tomatoes, chopped
- 1 cup fresh (or canned) corn
- ½ English cucumber, chopped
- ¼ red onion, chopped
- 1 tablespoon jalapeño pepper, chopped
- 1 tablespoon fresh cilantro, chopped
- Sea salt, for seasoning
- Freshly ground black pepper, for seasoning
- 1 pound extra-lean beef flank steak, trimmed of fat
- Olive oil, for brushing
- 1 teaspoon garlic powder
- 1 teaspoon chili powder

Directions:

1. Preheat the toaster oven to 450°F on BROIL for 5 minutes.

2. In a small bowl, stir the tomato, corn, cucumber, onion, jalapeño, and cilantro, and season with salt and pepper.

3. Rub the steak all over with the oil and then season with garlic powder, chili powder, salt, and pepper.

4. Place the air-fryer basket in the baking tray and arrange the steak in the basket.

5. In position 2, broil for 20 minutes, turning halfway through, until browned and with an internal temperature of 140°F, for medium-rare.

6. Let the steak rest for 10 minutes and then cut it very thinly against the grain.

7. Serve with the salsa.

Steak With Herbed Butter

Servings: 2

Cooking Time: 16 Minutes

Ingredients:

- 4 tablespoons unsalted butter, softened
- 1 tablespoon minced flat-leaf (Italian) parsley
- 1 tablespoon chopped fresh chives
- 2 cloves garlic, minced
- 1 teaspoon Worcestershire sauce
- 2 beef strip steaks, cut about 1 ½ inches thick
- 1 tablespoon olive oil
- Kosher salt and freshly ground black pepper

Directions:

1. Combine the butter, parsley, chives, garlic, and Worcestershire sauce in a small bowl until well blended; set aside.

2. Preheat the toaster oven to broil.

3. Brush the steaks with olive oil and season with salt and pepper. Place the steak on the broiler rack set over the broiler pan. Place the pan in the toaster oven, positioning the steaks about 3 to 4 inches below the heating element. (Depending on your oven and the thickness of the steak, you may need to set the rack to the middle position.) Broil for 6 minutes, turn the steaks over, and broil for an additional 7 minutes. If necessary to reach the desired doneness, turn the steaks over again and broil for an additional 3 minutes or until you reach your desired doneness.

4. Spread the herb butter generously over the steaks. Allow the steaks to stand for 5 to 10 minutes before slicing and serving.

Perfect Pork Chops

Servings: 3

Cooking Time: 10 Minutes

Ingredients:

- ¾ teaspoon Mild paprika
- ¾ teaspoon Dried thyme
- ¾ teaspoon Onion powder
- ¼ teaspoon Garlic powder
- ¼ teaspoon Table salt
- ¼ teaspoon Ground black pepper
- 3 6-ounce boneless center-cut pork loin chops
- Vegetable oil spray

Directions:

1. Preheat the toaster oven to 400°F.

2. Mix the paprika, thyme, onion powder, garlic powder, salt, and pepper in a small bowl until well combined. Massage this mixture into both sides of the chops. Generously coat both sides of the chops with vegetable oil spray.

3. When the machine is at temperature, set the chops in the air fryer oven with as much air space between them as possible. Air-fry undisturbed for 10 minutes, or until an instant-read meat thermometer inserted into the thickest part of a chop registers 145°F.

4. Use kitchen tongs to transfer the chops to a cutting board or serving plates. Cool for 5 minutes before serving.

Kielbasa Chunks With Pineapple & Peppers

Servings: 2

Cooking Time: 10 Minutes

Ingredients:

- ¾ pound kielbasa sausage
- 1 cup bell pepper chunks (any color)
- 1 8-ounce can pineapple chunks in juice, drained
- 1 tablespoon barbeque seasoning
- 1 tablespoon soy sauce
- cooking spray

Directions:

1. Cut sausage into ½-inch slices.

2. In a medium bowl, toss all ingredients together.

3. Spray air fryer oven with nonstick cooking spray.

4. Pour sausage mixture into the air fryer oven.

5. Air-fry at 390°F for approximately 5 minutes. Cook an additional 5 minutes.

Pretzel-coated Pork Tenderloin

Servings: 4

Cooking Time: 10 Minutes

Ingredients:

- 1 Large egg white(s)
- 2 teaspoons Dijon mustard (gluten-free, if a concern)
- 1½ cups (about 6 ounces) Crushed pretzel crumbs
- 1 pound (4 sections) Pork tenderloin, cut into ¼-pound (4-ounce) sections
- Vegetable oil spray

Directions:

1. Preheat the toaster oven to 350°F .

2. Set up and fill two shallow soup plates or small pie plates on your counter: one for the egg white(s), whisked with the mustard until foamy; and one for the pretzel crumbs.

3. Dip a section of pork tenderloin in the egg white mixture and turn it to coat well, even on the ends. Let any excess egg white mixture slip back into the rest, then set the pork in the pretzel crumbs. Roll it several times, pressing gently, until the pork is evenly coated, even on the ends. Generously coat the pork section with vegetable oil spray, set it aside, and continue coating and spraying the remaining sections.

4. Set the pork sections in the air fryer oven with at least ¼ inch between them. Air-fry undisturbed for 10 minutes, or until an instant-read meat thermometer inserted into the center of one section registers 145°F.

5. Use kitchen tongs to transfer the pieces to a wire rack. Cool for 3 to 5 minutes before serving.

Lime And Cumin Lamb Kebabs

Servings: 4

Cooking Time: 16 Minutes

Ingredients:

- 1 pound boneless lean lamb, trimmed and cut into 1 × 1-inch pieces
- 2 plum tomatoes, cut into 2 × 2-inch pieces
- 1 bell pepper, cut into 2 × 2-inch pieces
- 1 small onion, cut into 2 × 2-inch pieces
- Brushing mixture:
- ¼ cup lime juice
- ½ teaspoon soy sauce
- 1 tablespoon honey
- 1½ teaspoon ground cumin

Directions:

1. Skewer alternating pieces of lamb, tomato, pepper, and onion on four 9-inch skewers.

2. Combine the brushing mixture ingredients in a small bowl and brush on the kebabs. Place the skewers on a broiling rack with a pan underneath.

3. BROIL for 8 minutes. Turn the skewers, brush the kebabs with the mixture, and broil for 8 minutes, or until the meat and vegetables are cooked and browned.

Barbecue-style London Broil

Servings: 5

Cooking Time: 17 Minutes

Ingredients:

- ¾ teaspoon Mild smoked paprika
- ¾ teaspoon Dried oregano
- ¾ teaspoon Table salt
- ¾ teaspoon Ground black pepper
- ¼ teaspoon Garlic powder
- ¼ teaspoon Onion powder
- 1½ pounds Beef London broil (in one piece)
- Olive oil spray

Directions:

1. Preheat the toaster oven to 400°F.

2. Mix the smoked paprika, oregano, salt, pepper, garlic powder, and onion powder in a small bowl until uniform.

3. Pat and rub this mixture across all surfaces of the beef. Lightly coat the beef on all sides with olive oil spray.

4. When the machine is at temperature, lay the London broil flat in the air fryer oven and air-fry undisturbed for 8 minutes for the small batch, 10 minutes for the medium batch, or 12 minutes for the large batch for medium-rare, until an instant-read meat thermometer inserted into the center of the meat registers 130°F (not USDA-approved). Add 1, 2, or 3 minutes, respectively (based on the size of the cut) for medium, until an instant-read meat thermometer registers 135°F (not USDA-approved). Or add 3, 4, or 5 minutes respectively for medium, until an instant-read meat thermometer registers 145°F (USDA-approved).

5. Use kitchen tongs to transfer the London broil to a cutting board. Let the meat rest for 10 minutes. It needs a long time for the juices to be reincorporated into the meat's fibers. Carve it against the grain into very thin (less than ¼-inch-thick) slices to serve.

Beef Bourguignon

Servings: 6
Cooking Time: 240 Minutes

Ingredients:
- 4 slices bacon, chopped into ½-inch pieces
- 3 pounds chuck roast, cut into 2-inch chunks
- 1 tablespoon kosher salt, plus more to taste
- 1½ tablespoons black pepper, plus more to taste
- 4 tablespoons all purpose flour, divided
- 2 tablespoons olive oil
- 2 large carrots, cut into ½-inch thick slices
- ½ large white onion, diced
- 4 cloves garlic, minced
- 2 tablespoons tomato paste
- 3 cups red wine (Merlot, Pinot Noir, or Chianti)
- 2 cups beef stock
- 1 beef bouillon cube, crushed
- ½ teaspoon dried thyme
- ¼ teaspoon dried parsley
- 2 bay leaves
- 10 ounces fresh small white or brown mushrooms, quartered
- 2 tablespoons cornstarch (optional)
- 2 tablespoons water (optional)

Directions:
1. Render the bacon in a large pot over medium heat for 5 minutes or until crispy.

2. Drain the bacon and set aside, leaving the bacon fat in the pot.

3. Mix together chuck roast chunks, kosher salt, black pepper, and 2 tablespoons of all purpose flour until well combined.

4. Dredge the beef of any extra flour and sear in the bacon grease for about 4 minutes on each side. It is important not to overcrowd the pot, so you may need to work in batches.

5. Remove the beef when done and set aside with the bacon.

6. Add the olive oil, sliced carrots, and diced onion to the pot. Cook for 5 minutes, then add the garlic and cook for another minute.

7. Add the tomato paste and cook for 1 minute, then mix in the remaining 2 tablespoons of flour and cook on medium low for 4 minutes.

8. Pour in the wine and beef stock, scraping the bottom of the pot to make sure there aren't any bits stuck to the bottom.

9. Add the bacon and seared meat back into the pot, along with the bouillon cube, dried thyme, dried parsley, bay leaves, and mushrooms. Mix well and bring to a light boil.

10. Insert the wire rack at low position in the Air Fryer Toaster Oven.

11. Cover the pot with foil and place on the rack in the oven. Make sure the foil is secure so it doesn't lift and contact the heating elements.

12. Select the Slow Cook function, adjust time to 4 hours, and press Start/Pause.

13. Remove the pot carefully from the oven when done and place back on the stove.

14. Discard the foil, mix the stew, and season to taste with salt and pepper.

15. Thicken the stew if desired by using a cornstarch slurry of 2 tablespoons cornstarch and 2 tablespoons water. Add half, mix, and bring to a boil, stirring occasionally. If the sauce is still too thin, add the other half of the slurry.

Pesto Pork Chops

Servings: 2

Cooking Time: 15 Minutes

Ingredients:

- 2 (6-ounce) boneless pork loin chops
- 2 tablespoons basil pesto

Directions:

1. Preheat the toaster oven to 375°F on AIR FRY for 5 minutes.

2. Rub the pork chops all over with the pesto and set aside for 15 minutes.

3. Place the air-fryer basket in the baking tray and arrange the pork in the basket with no overlap.

4. In position 2, air fry for 15 minutes, turning halfway through, until the chops are lightly browned and have an internal temperature of 145°F.

5. Let the meat rest for 10 minutes and serve.

Lamb Koftas Meatballs

Servings: 3

Cooking Time: 8 Minutes

Ingredients:

- 1 pound ground lamb
- 1 teaspoon ground cumin
- 1 teaspoon ground coriander
- 2 tablespoons chopped fresh mint
- 1 egg, beaten
- ½ teaspoon salt
- freshly ground black pepper

Directions:

1. Combine all ingredients in a bowl and mix together well. Divide the mixture into 10 portions. Roll each portion into a ball and then by cupping the meatball in your hand, shape it into an oval.

2. Preheat the toaster oven to 400°F.

3. Air-fry the koftas for 8 minutes.

4. Serve warm with the cucumber-yogurt dip.

Orange Glazed Pork Tenderloin

Servings: 3

Cooking Time: 23 Minutes

Ingredients:

- 2 tablespoons brown sugar
- 2 teaspoons cornstarch
- 2 teaspoons Dijon mustard
- ½ cup orange juice
- ½ teaspoon soy sauce
- 2 teaspoons grated fresh ginger
- ¼ cup white wine
- zest of 1 orange
- 1 pound pork tenderloin
- salt and freshly ground black pepper
- oranges, halved (for garnish)
- fresh parsley or other green herb (for garnish)

Directions:

1. Combine the brown sugar, cornstarch, Dijon mustard, orange juice, soy sauce, ginger, white wine and orange zest in a small saucepan and bring the mixture to a boil on the stovetop. Lower the heat and simmer while you cook the pork tenderloin or until the sauce has thickened.

2. Preheat the toaster oven to 370°F.

3. Season all sides of the pork tenderloin with salt and freshly ground black pepper. Transfer the tenderloin to the air fryer oven, bending the pork into a wide "U" shape if necessary to fit in the air fryer oven. Air-fry at 370°F for 20 to 23 minutes, or until the internal temperature reaches 145°F. Flip the tenderloin over halfway through the cooking process and baste with the sauce.

4. Transfer the tenderloin to a cutting board and let it rest for 5 minutes. Slice the pork at a slight angle and serve immediately with orange halves and fresh herbs to dress it up. Drizzle any remaining glaze over the top.

Beer-baked Pork Tenderloin

Servings: 4

Cooking Time: 40 Minutes

Ingredients:

- 1 pound lean pork tenderloin, fat trimmed off
- 3 garlic cloves, minced
- 1 cup good-quality dark ale or beer
- 2 bay leaves
- Salt and freshly cracked black pepper
- Spiced apple slices

Directions:

1. Preheat the toaster oven to 400° F.

2. Place the tenderloin in an 8½ × 8½ × 4-inch ovenproof baking dish. Sprinkle the minced garlic over the pork, pour over the beer, add the bay leaves, and season to taste with the salt and pepper. Cover with aluminum foil.

3. BAKE, covered, for 40 minutes, or until the meat is tender. Discard the bay leaves and serve sliced with the liquid. Garnish with the spiced apple slices.

Beef And Spinach Braciole

Servings: 4

Cooking Time: 92 Minutes

Ingredients:

- 7-inch oven-safe baking pan or casserole

- ½ onion, finely chopped
- 1 teaspoon olive oil
- ⅓ cup red wine
- 2 cups crushed tomatoes
- 1 teaspoon Italian seasoning
- ½ teaspoon garlic powder
- ¼ teaspoon crushed red pepper flakes
- 2 tablespoons chopped fresh parsley
- 2 top round steaks (about 1½ pounds)
- salt and freshly ground black pepper
- 2 cups fresh spinach, chopped
- 1 clove minced garlic
- ½ cup roasted red peppers, julienned
- ½ cup grated pecorino cheese
- ¼ cup pine nuts, toasted and rough chopped
- 2 tablespoons olive oil

Directions:

1. Preheat the toaster oven to 400°F.

2. Toss the onions and olive oil together in a 7-inch metal baking pan or casserole dish. Air-fry at 400°F for 5 minutes, stirring a couple times during the cooking process. Add the red wine, crushed tomatoes, Italian seasoning, garlic powder, red pepper flakes and parsley and stir. Cover the pan tightly with aluminum foil, lower the air fryer oven temperature to 350°F and continue to air-fry for 15 minutes.

3. While the sauce is simmering, prepare the beef. Using a meat mallet, pound the beef until it is ¼-inch thick. Season both sides of the beef with salt and pepper. Combine the spinach, garlic, red peppers, pecorino cheese, pine nuts and olive oil in a medium bowl. Season with salt and freshly ground black pepper. Spread the mixture evenly over the steaks. Starting at one of the short ends, roll the beef around the filling, tucking in the sides as you roll to ensure the filling is completely enclosed. Secure the beef rolls with toothpicks.

4. Remove the baking pan with the sauce from the air fryer oven and set it aside. Preheat the toaster oven to 400°F.

5. Brush or spray the beef rolls with a little olive oil and air-fry at 400°F for 12 minutes, rotating the beef during the cooking process for even browning. When the beef is browned, submerge the rolls into the sauce in the baking pan, cover the pan with foil and return it to the air fryer oven. Air-fry at 250°F for 60 minutes.

6. Remove the beef rolls from the sauce. Cut each roll into slices and serve with pasta, ladling some of the sauce overtop.

Sweet Potato–crusted Pork Rib Chops

Servings: 2

Cooking Time: 14 Minutes

Ingredients:

- 2 Large egg white(s), well beaten
- 1½ cups (about 6 ounces) Crushed sweet potato chips (certified gluten-free, if a concern)
- 1 teaspoon Ground cinnamon
- 1 teaspoon Ground dried ginger
- 1 teaspoon Table salt (optional)
- 2 10-ounce, 1-inch-thick bone-in pork rib chop(s)

Directions:

1. Preheat the toaster oven to 375°F .

2. Set up and fill two shallow soup plates or small pie plates on your counter: one for the beaten egg white(s); and one for the crushed chips, mixed with the cinnamon, ginger, and salt (if using).

3. Dip a chop in the egg white(s), coating it on both sides as well as the edges. Let the excess egg white slip back into the rest, then set it in the crushed chip mixture. Turn it several times, pressing gently, until evenly coated on both sides and the edges. If necessary, set the chop aside and coat the remaining chop(s).

4. Set the chop(s) in the air fryer oven with as much air space between them as possible. Air-fry undisturbed for 12 minutes, or until crunchy and browned and an instant-read meat thermometer inserted into the center of a chop (without touching bone) registers 145°F. If the machine is at 360°F, you may need to add 2 minutes to the cooking time.

5. Use kitchen tongs to transfer the chop(s) to a wire rack. Cool for 2 or 3 minutes before serving.

Bourbon Broiled Steak

Servings: 2

Cooking Time: 14 Minutes

Ingredients:

- Brushing mixture:
- ¼ cup bourbon
- 1 teaspoon garlic powder
- 1 tablespoon olive oil
- 1 teaspoon soy sauce
- 2 6- to 8-ounce sirloin steaks, ¾ inch thick

Directions:

1. Combine the brushing mixture ingredients in a small bowl. Brush the steaks on both sides with the mixture and place on the broiling rack with a pan underneath.

2. BROIL 4 minutes, remove from the oven, turn with tongs, brush the top and sides, and broil again for 4 minutes, or until done to your preference. To use the brushing mixture as a sauce or gravy, pour the mixture into a baking pan.

3. BROIL the mixture for 6 minutes, or until it begins to bubble.

Kielbasa Sausage With Pierogies And Caramelized Onions

Servings: 3

Cooking Time: 30 Minutes

Ingredients:

- 1 Vidalia or sweet onion, sliced
- olive oil
- salt and freshly ground black pepper
- 2 tablespoons butter, cut into small cubes
- 1 teaspoon sugar
- 1 pound light Polish kielbasa sausage, cut into 2-inch chunks
- 1 (13-ounce) package frozen mini pierogies
- 2 teaspoons vegetable or olive oil
- chopped scallions

Directions:

1. Preheat the toaster oven to 400°F.

2. Toss the sliced onions with a little olive oil, salt and pepper and transfer them to the air fryer oven. Dot the onions with pieces of butter and air-fry at 400°F for 2 minutes. Then sprinkle the sugar over the onions and stir. Pour any melted butter from the bottom of the air fryer oven over the onions (do this over the sink – some of the butter will spill through the pan). Continue to air-fry for another 13 minutes, stirring the pan every few minutes to cook the onions evenly.

3. Add the kielbasa chunks to the onions and toss. Air-fry for another 5 minutes. Transfer the kielbasa and onions to a bowl and cover with aluminum foil to keep warm.

4. Toss the frozen pierogies with the vegetable or olive oil and transfer them to the air fryer oven. Air-fry at 400°F for 8 minutes.

5. When the pierogies have finished cooking, return the kielbasa and onions to the air fryer oven and gently toss with the pierogies. Air-fry for 2 more minutes and then transfer everything to a serving platter. Garnish with the chopped scallions and serve hot with the spicy sour cream sauce below.

6. Kielbasa Sausage with Pierogies and Caramelized Onions

Lamb Curry

Servings: 4
Cooking Time: 40 Minutes

Ingredients:
- 1 pound lean lamb for stewing, trimmed and cut into 1 × 1-inch pieces
- 1 small onion, chopped
- 3 garlic cloves, minced
- 2 plum tomatoes, chopped
- ½ cup dry white wine
- 2 tablespoons curry powder
- Salt and cayenne to taste

Directions:
1. Preheat the toaster oven to 400° F.
2. Combine all the ingredients in an 8½ × 8½ × 4-inch ovenproof baking dish. Adjust the seasonings.
3. BAKE, covered, for 40 minutes, or until the meat is tender and the onion is cooked.

Vietnamese Beef Lettuce Wraps

Servings: 4
Cooking Time: 12 Minutes

Ingredients:
- ⅓ cup low-sodium soy sauce
- 2 teaspoons fish sauce
- 2 teaspoons brown sugar
- 1 tablespoon chili paste
- juice of 1 lime
- 2 cloves garlic, minced
- 2 teaspoons fresh ginger, minced
- 1 pound beef sirloin
- Sauce
- ⅓ cup low-sodium soy sauce
- juice of 2 limes
- 1 tablespoon mirin wine
- 2 teaspoons chili paste
- Serving
- 1 head butter lettuce

- ½ cup julienned carrots
- ½ cup julienned cucumber
- ½ cup sliced radishes, sliced into half moons
- 2 cups cooked rice noodles
- ⅓ cup chopped peanuts

Directions:

1. Combine the soy sauce, fish sauce, brown sugar, chili paste, lime juice, garlic and ginger in a bowl. Slice the beef into thin slices, then cut those slices in half. Add the beef to the marinade and marinate for 1 to 3 hours in the refrigerator. When you are ready to cook, remove the steak from the refrigerator and let it sit at room temperature for 30 minutes.

2. Preheat the toaster oven to 400°F.

3. Transfer the beef and marinade to the air fryer oven. Air-fry at 400°F for 12 minutes.

4. While the beef is cooking, prepare a wrap-building station. Combine the soy sauce, lime juice, mirin wine and chili paste in a bowl and transfer to a little pouring vessel. Separate the lettuce leaves from the head of lettuce and put them in a serving bowl. Place the carrots, cucumber, radish, rice noodles and chopped peanuts all in separate serving bowls.

5. When the beef has finished cooking, transfer it to another serving bowl and invite your guests to build their wraps. To build the wraps, place some beef in a lettuce leaf and top with carrots, cucumbers, some rice noodles and chopped peanuts. Drizzle a little sauce over top, fold the lettuce around the ingredients and enjoy!

Slow Cooked Carnitas

Servings: 6

Cooking Time: 360 Minutes

Ingredients:

- 1 pork shoulder (5 pounds), bone-in
- 2½ teaspoons kosher salt
- 1½ teaspoons black pepper
- 1½ teaspoons ground cumin
- 1 teaspoon dried oregano
- ¼ teaspoon ground coriander
- 2 bay leaves
- 6 garlic cloves
- 1 small onion, quartered
- 1 cinnamon stick
- 1 full orange peel (no white)
- 2 oranges, juiced
- 1 lime, juiced

Directions:

1. Season the pork shoulder with salt, pepper, cumin, oregano, and coriander.

2. Place the seasoned pork shoulder in a large pot along with any seasoning that did not stick to the pork.

3. Add in the bay leaves, garlic cloves, onion, cinnamon stick, and orange peel.

4. Squeeze in the juice of two oranges and one lime and cover with foil.

5. Insert the wire rack at low position in the Air Fryer Toaster Oven, then place the pot on the rack.

6. Select the Slow Cook function and press Start/Pause.

7. Remove carefully when done, uncover, and remove the bone.

8. Shred the carnitas and use them in tacos, burritos, or any other way you please.

Zesty London Broil

Servings: 4

Cooking Time: 28 Minutes

Ingredients:

- ⅔ cup ketchup
- ¼ cup honey
- ¼ cup olive oil
- 2 tablespoons apple cider vinegar
- 2 tablespoons Worcestershire sauce
- 2 tablespoons minced onion
- ½ teaspoon paprika
- 1 teaspoon salt
- 1 teaspoon freshly ground black pepper
- 2 pounds London broil, top round or flank steak (about 1-inch thick)

Directions:

1. Combine the ketchup, honey, olive oil, apple cider vinegar, Worcestershire sauce, minced onion, paprika, salt and pepper in a small bowl and whisk together.

2. Generously pierce both sides of the meat with a fork or meat tenderizer and place it in a shallow dish. Pour the marinade mixture over the steak, making sure all sides of the meat get coated with the marinade. Cover and refrigerate overnight.

3. Preheat the toaster oven to 400°F.

4. Transfer the London broil to the air fryer oven and air-fry for 28 minutes, depending on how rare or well done you like your steak. Flip the steak over halfway through the cooking time.

5. Remove the London broil from the air fryer oven and let it rest for five minutes on a cutting board. To serve, thinly slice the meat against the grain and transfer to a serving platter.